God's Ordinary Giants

Discover Your Role in Advancing God's Kingdom

French B. Harmon

Sermon To Book
www.sermontobook.com

God's Ordinary Giants / French B. Harmon
ISBN-13: 978-1-952602-31-3

This book is dedicated to my wife and life partner, Rachael. I am forever grateful for every sacrifice made to advance God's Kingdom on our journey. May the Lord bless you for being such a great and loving mother to our children—Trae, Madison, and Jack.

CONTENTS

People—Just Like Us 3

Paul—A Coaching Legend 13

John—A Passionate Believer 29

Barnabas—A Great Encourager 43

James—The Practical Christian..............................55

Luke—A Gifted Person 71

Matthew—The Unpopular One 83

Thomas—The Discouraged Christian 95

John Mark—A Quitter..107

Peter—The Courageous One 121

Philip—The Inviter...133

Timothy—The Young Christian.............................147

Stephen—The Risk Taker.......................................161

Aquila and Priscilla— Believers Who Loved the Church...175

Nicodemus— The One Who Desired Real Faith 187

Joseph—A Father of Character 199

Mary—A Devoted Mother 211

People of Excellence..225

Walk in Faith 241

About the Author 245

About Sermon To Book..247

Notes..249

People—Just Like Us

Have you ever felt you're adrift on the sea without a captain? Or, perhaps, that God is calling you to step up and do something significant in your spiritual life. Each of us longs to accomplish something of value—to make our impact on the world in which we live. Our desire might be to help others find their way safely to shore, but we can't seem to find a place of smooth sailing amidst the waves that toss us back and forth. All around, we observe others who steer a steady course and wonder how we might emulate their courageous actions.

Humanity longs for personal significance—a way to make a difference. Often, we look to others for examples of how to fulfill these longings when their lifestyle, work, or contributions to society seem to be significant. In an attempt to be better Christians, we observe those around us for actions and behaviors that will *up our game* for God. We might even view those people as *giants*—larger than life in what they are able to accomplish in their spiritual lives. Yet, within each person lies the very image of

God (Genesis 1:27). He has given us unique gifts and talents and wants us to do our best for Him.

In our current culture of creature comforts, we give up at the first sign of difficulty. At the first sign of gale force winds and crashing waves, we're ready to bail. If the first mate rubs us the wrong way, we're ready to try another church. Is that being a steadfast sailor, as God calls each of us to be?

God wants to help us take control in spiritual situations and to use our talents and strengths for Him. Paul experienced shipwrecks in life, and so do we. We may feel abandoned in the faith, but the Lord encourages us to set forth again, realizing we have a life of great potential.

How can recognizing God as our captain help us live a life of significance? In the Bible, God gives us examples of amazing leaders whom we can emulate. God uses many different people to build His kingdom; we are not all the same, and He uses all of our gifts for His glory. God's giants are not superhumans with the strength to take over the world, the size to win contests of physical skill, or the power to intimidate the masses. They are ordinary people like us, inspired by God to reach the ultimate destination—His kingdom of love—one step at a time.

The Bible tells many stories of ordinary people who did extraordinary things in God's strength. Because they lived many years ago in a different culture, it's easy to put these biblical characters on a pedestal and not feel any sort of connection with them. But they are people, just like us. Let's not forget they struggled with many of the same issues we face. However, they believed God would help them through rough waters. In observing the lives of these saints in the faith, we can rise up to be leaders, giants in our generation. God calls and uses a wide variety of people throughout the Bible. Some are brave, fierce fighters and others are cowards who run away. Yet, God calls them all! Even Jesus' own disciples were a motley group. These men were both hot-tempered and calm, quick to give answers yet totally confused, daring while terrified. But they were used as part of God's plan to start the church. The Book of Acts and Paul's epistles paint a picture of all sorts of people called together to walk as giants and leaders in their communities to advance God's kingdom.

When we think of someone who is a giant, we often think of a person who is larger than life with superhuman abilities or power to perform incredible and mighty things. Our images of giants typically include characteristics of great strength, intellect, or ability.

Ordinary giants in the Bible are people who had a strong faith in Jesus and lived it out in practical ways. James, the brother of Jesus, lived a simple, practical faith for all to see. In faith, Peter stepped out of his comfort zone; he called out to Jesus in faith when he started to sink. Stephen's faith was so strong he risked everything and was martyred for his devotion to Jesus (Acts 7:54–60).

We also see people looking up to the ordinary giants of the New Testament because of their great intellect or spiritual wisdom. Luke, a gifted physician, used what God had given him to glorify God and reach others for Christ. John Mark had great training and humbled himself to come back to God after he failed. Philip and Nicodemus longed to learn more about Jesus and His kingdom; they knew what they didn't know and reached out to God. Mary accepted all God had for her from a place of openness and spiritual sensitivity. And Joseph guided his family with wisdom as he followed God first.

These ordinary men and women in the Bible used their God-given gifts and abilities to do great things for Him. Paul was a gifted coach who taught with wisdom and then helped believers apply spiritual lessons to all aspects of their lives. God gave Barnabas a tremendous gift of encouragement that enabled him to accept people and think of others first to help them in *their* ministries. Aquila and Priscilla used their gifts of hospitality and of loving people to spread the gospel message wherever they lived.

Other ordinary giants in the New Testament went above and beyond what we'd expect. John's passion for Christ led him to love Jesus deeply and write eloquently about what it means to believe in God. Matthew and Thomas, even though they faced challenges in their Christian walks, were willing to let Jesus transform their lives in extraordinary ways. Even though he was young, Timothy played a vital role in Paul's ministry, as he served and became an example of a devoted follower of Christ.

It doesn't matter if you are a bold, passionate Christian; an experienced, wise Christian; a timid, fearful Christian; or uncertain whether you want to be a Christian at all. These stories of the men and women whom God chose to be part of his ragtag group of followers are for us. In this book, we will explore their stories and learn from their lives. At the end of each chapter, workbook sections will help you take the lessons from each of these ordinary giants and apply them to your own life in relevant and meaningful ways.

By understanding the lives of these ordinary giants of faith, we will discover the role God intends for each of us to play in advancing His kingdom. Let's consider our strengths and weaknesses as we answer the call to become more like Jesus, a gentle giant who led people into closer relationship with our heavenly Father.

WORKBOOK

Introduction Questions

Question: Who are some people, either from the Bible or Christian history, whom you consider giants in the faith? What made their lives so significant? In what ways were they just ordinary people who allowed God to use them?

_____

_____

_____

_____

_____

_____

_____

_____

_____

_____

Question: How do you dream of using your God-given gifts and talents for Christ? How do you hope to make a difference for Him in the world?

_____

_____

_____

_____

_____

_____

_____

_____

_____

_____

_____

Question: What obstacles do you feel stand in the way of living a life of surrender and significance? Is God the captain of your life or are you trying to navigate through life in your own wisdom and ability?

_____

_____

_____

_____

_____

_____

_____

_____

_____

_____

_____

_____

Action: Jot down some of your gifts and how you could use them for the Lord. If you are not sure of your spiritual gifts or natural abilities, there are many assessment tools that can help you in determining the unique ways that you can serve God and bless others.

Introduction Notes

_____

_____

_____

_____

_____

_____

_____

_____

_____

_____

_____

_____

_____

_____

_____

_____

_____

_____

_____

_____

_____

CHAPTER ONE

Paul—A Coaching Legend

Rejoice in the Lord always. I will say it again: Rejoice! Let your gentleness be evident to all. The Lord is near. Do not be anxious about anything, but in every situation, by prayer and petition, with thanksgiving, present your requests to God. And the peace of God, which transcends all understanding, will guard your hearts and your minds in Christ Jesus.

Finally, brothers and sisters, whatever is true, whatever is noble, whatever is right, whatever is pure, whatever is lovely, whatever is admirable—if anything is excellent or praiseworthy—think about such things. Whatever you have learned or received or heard from me, or seen in me— put it into practice. And the God of peace will be with you.

I rejoiced greatly in the Lord that at last you renewed your concern for me. Indeed, you were concerned, but you had no opportunity to show it. I am not saying this because I am in need, for I have learned to be content whatever the circumstances. I know what it is to be in need, and I know what it is to have plenty. I have learned the secret of being content in any and every situation, whether well fed or hungry, whether living in plenty or in want. I can do all this through him who gives me strength.
—Philippians 4:4–13

Our society often looks up to coaches as giants: people who are larger than life because they lead a team to greatness and victory. A coach doesn't play the game but, instead, leads by helping others play better. Coaches impart philosophy, knowledge, skills, and strategies to guide teams to success. They help players apply lessons learned through sports to other aspects of their lives. Coaches encourage their players and build strong bonds with them.[1]

Lessons from Paul

Many view Paul as a legendary Christian and pastor. He became a church coach who wanted to get the best out of his team and his players—his fellow Christians. Paul helped church after church, member after member, Christian after Christian, encouraging them and building strong bonds through personal visits and letters. Paul wrote from the sidelines of prison to help others play the game in such a way to win the victory. His writing gives readers understanding and tips—skills and strategies—to live successful Christian lives. Paul is a spiritual giant, or a legendary coach, because his influence continues to this day.

In his letter to the believers at Philippi, Paul inserts coaching tips for practical application: "Whatever you have learned or received or heard from me, or seen in me—put it into practice. And the God of peace will be with you" (Philippians 4:9). Paul is the coach reminding us, his team, to emulate godly behavior. Farther down in the same passage, he says, "I can do all things through him who gives me strength" (Philippians 4:13). Paul expresses his complete dependence on God for a victorious life. In this same way, his reminder for us today is that nothing is impossible—including putting these coaching tips into practice in our lives.

Paul coaches us to trust our hearts and minds to God. Twenty years ago, I was in a different place. I had cancer, and every single day, sometimes multiple times a day, I would recite the following passage, because when things get tough, we can't give in. These verses had a great impact on me during my illness:

> *Rejoice in the Lord always. I will say it again: Rejoice! Let your gentleness be evident to all. The Lord is near. Do not be anxious about anything, but in every situation, by prayer and petition, with thanksgiving, present your requests to God. And the peace of God, which transcends all understanding, will guard your hearts and your minds in Christ Jesus.*
> **—Philippians 4:4–7**

Satan may try to take your mind or heart, but Paul tells us that if we give our hearts and minds to God, He will guard them. This coaching tip applies to each of us. When things get hard, don't complain; rejoice! Don't get negative; get positive! Always offer yourself—mind, body, and spirit—to God in prayer.

Paul exhorts believers to "rejoice in the Lord always," in your good times and bad (Philippians 4:4). He also writes: "Let your gentleness be evident to all" (Philippians 4:5). Gentleness is a state of mind as well as a physical attribute. When fierce winds threaten to knock us down through the words or actions of others, gentleness allows us to remain calm and humble. For example, we are not to lash out because someone criticizes Jesus. Why would we? God is God, and whether others realize it or not, that's not going to change whether God is God. If someone criticizes Jesus Christ, let your gentleness be known. When you're a Christian, it doesn't change your opinion of God, because you know Him so well.

Maintaining an attitude of rejoicing and a focus on God helps us to have the peace of God. In today's world, people tend to look for peace in all the wrong places. It's true we might experience peace during quiet moments or while we are outside enjoying the beauty of nature, but those fleeting instances don't bring us the deep, inner peace Paul describes. True peace comes only from God. When our hearts and minds are trusted to God, we can experience peace in a supernatural way!

Paul coaches us to stay rooted firmly in the gospel (Colossians 2:7). Paul encourages us to turn to God in all things: "Do not be anxious about anything, but in every situation, by prayer and petition, with thanksgiving, present your requests to God" (Philippians 4:6). Go back to the fundamentals. It's about a relationship between you and God. When we have a bad day, God knows it and is there with us. Reach out to Him in the midst of difficult times. I know a woman who's already had cancer twice and is going through treatment again now. Another woman is in the middle of a tough journey, as she has traveled home to be with her parents, both critically ill and on the verge of death. I know teenagers going through unheard of health issues, but you'd never know it, because they're depending on God.

The word *gospel* comes to us from the Old English and means "good story" or "good news."[2] Paul writes in his letter to believers in Rome that he is "not ashamed of the gospel, because it is the power of God that brings salvation to everyone who believes" (Romans 1:16). We become rooted in Jesus Christ when we believe in the good news of salvation. Jesus told Nicodemus, one of the religious rulers, that He came to save the world, and that "whoever believes in him shall not perish but have eternal life" (John 3:16–18). Once we believe, He marks us "with a seal, the promised Holy Spirit" (Ephesians 1:13). Jesus says we are born of the Spirit or born again (John 3:6). We stay rooted to the gospel when we remind ourselves, *I've been born again.*

When we stay rooted firmly in the good news that God has the power and ability to save us from sin and bring us back to Himself, we practice Paul's next coaching tip here in Philippians.

Finally, brothers and sisters, whatever is true, whatever is noble, whatever is right, whatever is pure, whatever is lovely, whatever is admirable—if anything is excellent or praiseworthy—think about such things.
—Philippians 4:8

How you think is important. If you think negative thoughts, you'll be a negative person. When you are around negative people, it will rub off on you. God wants us to train our minds to think good thoughts, based on His thoughts, ways, and words.

One place where positive thinking directly impacts

people is in the hospital. As part of my pastoral duties, I regularly visit and pray with people who are sick or recovering from surgery or illness. Thinking you're going to get better is part of the healing process. And turning our hearts to God during difficult times helps us focus on those positive outcomes. Thanking God for His gracious gift of salvation keeps us firmly rooted in the gospel.

Paul coaches us to remain dedicated to the gospel. A lot of people are dedicated to different things—sports, civic organizations, programs, lifestyle. But the number one dedication of all Christians should be to the gospel of the One who gave His own life so we might have eternal life—Jesus Christ. Our dedication to the gospel grows from being rooted in the good news of salvation. How dedicated are we to His gospel? Are we dedicated to helping other people be saved?

I'm convinced we, as a Christian community, have lost our edge in sharing our faith. We strive so hard to make sure we don't offend anyone that we've watered down the gospel message. We don't say there's a need for all *to be saved*; we say there's a need for all *to believe*. You know what? We do need to be saved, because without Jesus Christ, we are eternally lost. Without Him, we're bound for a devil's hell—separation from God and His goodness forever (2 Thessalonians 1:9–10). It's more than believing. We're lost, but here's the great news: we have the opportunity to give our hearts and lives to Jesus Christ. Through Him, we can be found in God. He will carry away all our past sins; every sin we've ever committed can be wiped clean. We can go forward in life with a better plan, knowing we have a better home awaiting us. This is good news for everyone: we can be saved!

Paul said, "I am not ashamed of the gospel" (Romans 1:16). He was dedicated to knowing and living the gospel. We can't change anyone; we can't save anyone. Only Jesus can save, but our task is to present the good news. Being dedicated to the gospel, like Paul, is an important part of our Christian life.

What Is the Good News?

"For all have sinned and fall short of the glory of God" (Romans 3:23). We have a problem—it's called a sin problem. We all need to be saved.

"For the wages of sin is death" (Romans 6:23). Because we've sinned, we have been separated from God by our sin. But here's the good news: "God demonstrates his own love for us in this: While we were still sinners, Christ died for us" (Romans 5:8).

"Everyone who calls on the name of the Lord will be saved" (Romans 10:13). We may be dedicated to our local church, but that doesn't mean we're Christians. If you were to pass from this life to the next today, would you spend eternity in heaven? Or would it be in that other place? There's a heaven, and Paul was dedicated to making sure every person heard the gospel.

Paul coaches every one of us to be dedicated; we either are, or we aren't. Having done some coaching myself over the years, I know it's important to build dedication among the team. For instance, we might have early practices to determine their level of commitment. Sometimes, God may ask us to do some things we're uncomfortable doing. You know what He's great at? He puts us in uncomfortable situations sometimes to see if we're ashamed of Him or not. God gives us opportunities to show our dedication to Him and to the gospel.

I had this opportunity on a recent flight. The guy sitting beside me was a non-Christian. Within the first minute he asked, "What do you do?" When he heard I was a pastor, I could tell he was thinking, "*I'm going to have to spend two hours with this guy and he's going to try to convert me the whole time.*" But it was a fantastic conversation, with him leading the conversation and asking questions. When we're dedicated to the gospel—not to the church or to the pastor—God will give us opportunities to share our faith, and we will be blessed.

Paul was determined to be bold. He wasn't going to let opportunities pass him. He understood the truth he wrote in this passage to the Philippians. He wanted us all to realize we can come to God with anything. God is the answer. Drugs aren't the answer. Relationships alone aren't the answer. Jesus is the answer.

Many Christians are wishy-washy. It may take fifty gallons to baptize a Christian, but it may take only fifty drops of rain to keep a Christian away on the Lord's day! We need to be bold, but I'm afraid we've watered down some of our experiences in Christ. Our boldness has taken a back seat to our comfort level.

Paul coaches us to be dependent on the Holy Spirit. Paul was dependent on the Holy Spirit in every situation.

We have the Father, the Son, and the Holy Spirit—the Holy Trinity. They're all connected, three in one, one in three. Some people identify God the Father as the biggest, or most important, and Jesus and the Holy Spirit as smaller and less important. Others elevate the Holy Spirit, relegating Jesus to an ancillary part of the Trinity and diminishing God the Father. Still others make Jesus bigger than the Father and the Holy Spirit and choose to hardly acknowledge the Holy Spirit's presence. We all think we can do it on our own, preferring to create a version of the Trinity that fits our own needs and desires.

The Father, the Son, and the Holy Spirit are equal. They are the holy Trinity. We are instructed to pray to the Father in the power of the Spirit (Ephesians 6:18). Paul was dependent upon the Spirit to do the work. He was saved by Jesus but filled with the Spirit. The moment we choose to believe, we are filled with the Holy Spirit (Matthew 3:11, Acts 2:38). It's not a question of whether we have the Spirit. The question is, does the Holy Spirit have us? Are we dependent on Him? Are we walking in the Spirit (Galatians 5:16)? Are we being compelled by the Spirit to do His will?

Two weeks ago, I prayed over five or six young people and encouraged them to go out and be missionaries for the Lord. One person came to me later and said, "You'll never guess what happened—that same afternoon God gave me an incredible opportunity to serve Him." I believe in divine appointments. Don't underestimate the power of the Holy Spirit in the lives of believers.

Paul, our coach, gets straight to the point: if we're dedicated to the gospel, willing to be bold and dependent on the Holy Spirit, we can rest in the power provided to us. He's going to do some amazing things through His people.

Walking in Paul's Footsteps

Two-thirds of the way through our focus passage, Paul says, "Whatever you have learned or received or heard from me, or seen in me—put it into practice" (Philippians 4:9). He's like a soccer coach who sets up a drill during practice and then runs the course first to show his players how to do it. As the coach runs the course, he offers tips to his team for successful completion. Listening to and applying valuable insights from coaches like Paul helps us understand how to better live the Christian life as giants for God.

Paul's first tip is to trust our hearts and minds to God through prayer. Paul encourages us to pray in all situations (Ephesians 6:18; Philippians 4:6). God wants us to regularly come to Him and surrender all our thoughts and emotions.

Paul's next coaching tip is to stay rooted firmly in the gospel. We do this by spending time in God's Word. The best way to know who God is and how to follow Him is by reading what He has to say about Himself. It takes time for roots to grow deep, and when we plant ourselves in His Word, His truth stabilizes us.

The next coaching tip is related: remain dedicated to the gospel. With firmly established roots, we have the stability to reach out to others for God. Are you ready to dedicate your life to God, or do you want to be a part-time

Christian? God wants all of you.

Paul's final coaching tip is to be dependent on the Holy Spirit. Whenever worry strikes or temptation arises, we can call on the Holy Spirit. He will give us the strength, power, and endurance to do our best for God.

I want us to succeed as Christians. I want to see our churches succeed. I want to see us all win victories for our team. We must be dedicated to the gospel. We have to determine we'll be bold and dependent on the Holy Spirit. When we do, we'll see unbelievable blessings.

WORKBOOK

Chapter One Questions

Question: Describe a coach, either of a sports team or someone who mentored you in a life skill (such as a financial coach or a teacher/mentor), who made a difference in your life. What do you admire about this person, and why were they an influence on you? Have you had the opportunity to have that kind of influence on another person?

_____

_____

_____

_____

_____

_____

_____

_____

_____

Question: What are some circumstances that threaten your peace? In what ways does Satan try to attack your mind and your heart? How can you experience God's perfect peace even when the circumstances of life don't change and Satan's attacks don't stop?

_____

_____

_____

_____

_____

_____

_____

_____

_____

_____

_____

_____

Question: Recall your salvation testimony. When did you first hear the gospel? When did you first accept the truth of the gospel in a saving relationship with Jesus Christ? Are you devoted to the gospel—to boldly sharing it with those who need to hear it and to living a life that is totally dedicated to following God? Ask the Holy Spirit to give you both boldness and opportunities to share.

_____

_____

_____

_____

_____

_____

_____

_____

_____

_____

_____

_____

Action: Commit Philippians 4:4–7 to memory. When you are assaulted by fear or worry, begin to get off track about what really matters in life, or start hiding your faith instead of sharing it, prayerfully go back to Philippians 4:4–13.

Chapter One Notes

_____

_____

_____

_____

_____

_____

_____

_____

_____

_____

_____

_____

_____

_____

_____

_____

_____

_____

_____

_____

_____

_____

CHAPTER TWO

John—A Passionate Believer

...for everyone born of God overcomes the world. This is the victory that has overcome the world, even our faith. Who is it that overcomes the world? Only the one who believes that Jesus is the Son of God.

This is the one who came by water and blood—Jesus Christ. He did not come by water only, but by water and blood. And it is the Spirit who testifies, because the Spirit is the truth. For there are three that testify: the Spirit, the water and the blood; and the three are in agreement. We accept human testimony, but God's testimony is greater because it is the testimony of God, which he has given about his Son. Whoever believes in the Son of God accepts this testimony. Whoever does not believe God has made him out to be a liar, because they have not believed the testimony God has given about his Son. And this is the testimony: God has given us eternal life, and this life is in his Son. Whoever has the Son has life; whoever does not have the Son of God does not have life.

I write these things to you who believe in the name of the Son of God so that you may know that you have eternal life.
—1 John 5:4–13

We might not always look up to those in sales as giants or leaders in our society, but we have to admit we admire their passion. And sometimes, we need what they are selling, especially if we find ourselves in troubled waters. A primary example is technology. When something goes haywire with our computer or another device, we want someone knowledgeable to fix it right away. Even though many tech gurus are introverts, they are passionate about their work. If the technician knows the product, we are more likely to pay for their services, buy the latest piece of equipment, or upgrade. The salesperson is more likely to make the sale if he or she can convince us of the benefits of a particular product. Often, the salesperson's passion is the key to making the sale. Imagine how many people would be led to follow Jesus if we showed true passion for Him.

Lessons from John

John the apostle is a giant of faith. Before Jesus called him, John the apostle and his brother James were fishermen (Matthew 4:21). Note the difference between the two well-known men named *John* in the Bible. John the Baptist was Jesus' cousin, and John the apostle was the son of Zebedee. John the apostle stood at Jesus' feet, along with Jesus' mother Mary, when Jesus died (John 19:26–27). He wrote several books of the New Testament, including the Gospel of John and three letters. Because of his devotion to Christ, John was exiled to the Isle of Patmos, where he wrote the book of Revelation and eventually died (Revelation 1:9).

John was passionate. By the time we encounter him in his writing, he refers to himself as "the disciple whom Jesus loved" (John 13:23). The youngest of the apostles, John and his brother James were given the nickname Sons of Thunder (Mark 3:17). Apparently, others could rile John to such a point that he became thunderous. People knew where John stood concerning Jesus.

A passionate believer, John flamed the flames for Jesus. Enthusiasm goes a long way, whether in sports or theater or any other activity. If you're not enthusiastic, there's something missing on the inside. John was passionate from the inside out. He had a pure doctrine. His devotional life had purpose and he had a powerful message. The specific qualities John had as a passionate believer provide an example for us to follow if we want to become ordinary giants who lead others to Jesus.

John was passionate about salvation and shared a pure doctrine. A key component of John's doctrine, or teaching about God, is the importance of knowing that salvation cannot be lost (John 6:37–39). Christians refer to this as being eternally secure.

When I understood that once I became a Christian I'd never perish and I'd always be in God's hands, it changed my whole thinking about God. Some people believe it's possible to lose salvation, under the impression that we can be a Christian today yet be destined for hell if we do anything bad. We need to know even though there will be bad days, we are children of God (1 John 3:1). We'll always be His children, and He's not going to kick us out of the family. Once we grasp this truth, it changes the way we look at life!

There's a reason it's important to examine the doctrine of any church we commit to in attendance, fellowship, and ministry. Many churches align themselves as non-denominational. Jesus didn't get hung up on church names—they didn't have the specific denominational names we have now—but John does tell us what Jesus thought about doctrine. "Then you will know the truth, and the truth will set you free" (John 8:32). It's important to understand the concept of *once saved, always saved.* We declare our belief in this truth when we choose to follow Jesus in baptism. The act of being baptized doesn't save us, but it demonstrates to the world that we stand for Christ.

John wrote, "Whoever has the Son has life; whoever does not have the Son of God does not have life" (1 John 5:12). Does that resonate with you? A lot of people chase after all the wrong things. If we have Jesus, we have life here as well as in eternity. Once we have eternal life, we have life with God forever.

It's possible to know these things for a fact. In the next verse, John says, "I write these things … so that you may know that you have eternal life" (1 John 5:13). I want to underscore the word *know.* Can we absolutely know we have eternal life, that we are saved? What does this verse say? "So that you may know." God wants us to know we have eternal life and not just hope we have it. Some will say, "We can't really know anything." If that's true, this Book is false, because the Bible is the Word of God, 100 percent. Is it God's Word or not? If it's God's Word, every believer should memorize 1 John 5:13: "I write these things to you who believe … so that you may know that you have eternal life." We can place our soul, our whole understanding, in the sure knowledge that we have eternity with Christ as our future. God showed me what this means when I was seventeen or eighteen years old. As a freshman in college, I felt called to be a pastor. I began to study the Scriptures every day and night. A friend of mine who attended a different church said he had been saved thirty different times, because every time he committed a sin, he had to go back to the altar and get saved again.

I thought maybe that's what the Bible said and looked up the verses his pastor had given him. I discovered we *do* have to ask for forgiveness each time we sin, but not for purposes of salvation. This guy said we need to be saved again every time we sin. Sometimes, he would let his sins mount up a bit and then ask for forgiveness. In other words, he kept on sinning so he wouldn't have to give up a lot of things in his life!

My passion for God's truth spilled over, so in addition to His Word I also read all the great teachers of the faith. Adrian Rogers—a well-known American Southern Baptist pastor—wrote, "You'll see how rich you are when you add up everything you have that money can't buy, how much you have that death can't take away."[3] He taught eternal security and that we are wealthy in Christ. We don't need to struggle with our thoughts and feel the need to hold on to God. We're not big enough to hold onto God! God holds on to us. We are in the palm of His hand, not somehow holding on to Him. In John 10:28, Jesus says we're in the hands of God and no one can snatch us away. God's Spirit and the blood of Jesus Christ are so strong that Satan and this world cannot take away the relationship we have with almighty God (Romans 8:38–39)!

Doctrine—what we believe about God and what Jesus has done for us—is important. John had pure doctrine, built on the truth of God's Word. Once we are saved, we are always saved. We have eternal security through our relationship with Jesus Christ. We are saved forever, baptized into the body of Christ.

John was passionate about God's people and had a resolute devotion. John's devotion to Christ had a purpose. He was a giant of the faith, considered one of the three pillars of the church in Jerusalem. He was the one others would go to when they had issues. He was one of the pastors of the mother church where so much biblical history took place. Throughout the Book of Revelation, we see how John was in sync with God. The closer we walk with the Lord, the more it begins to manifest in our bearing, our face, and the way we view situations. Walking with God gives us purpose and power. When we walk with God, there's never a moment we should experience true fear.

As a pastor, I conduct a lot of funerals. I'm often around people who are about to face death. I've never met anyone in their thirties who thinks they're going to pass away. When I was in my twenties, I never gave it a thought. I'll never forget the largest funeral I ever preached—for a thirty-two-year-old principal. He was one of the most fantastic young Christians I've ever met. Beloved by those at his school, he died at a church athletic event. Everyone was crushed when his heart gave out. As I preached, the real question in the minds of the audience was, "Why?" I couldn't answer.

I meet with people in their seventies and eighties who ask me to preach at their funerals when the time comes. One person came from another city to ask me to preach at his funeral. While I'm honored to be asked, I said, "I'm humbled, but let's talk about living instead of dying."

We each need a purpose for our lives. Rick Warren, pastor of Saddleback Church, said, "Without God life has no purpose. And without purpose life has no meaning. Without meaning life has no significance or hope."[4] God wants us to have a life of purpose and significance.

John lived a passionate life, one with meaning and purpose, because he desired it and remained committed to his calling. He led the church in Jerusalem and became an institution. He didn't just pastor—he wrote, he taught, and he became an evangelist. He had a passion, a desire, and a determination to live a life of purpose throughout his life.

I knew a young teacher in Cincinnati who would arrive to his classroom a half hour early and walk the classroom, putting his hand on each desk and praying for each student by name. He was beloved, and he saw several young people come to Christ. We show we care about people when we invest in their lives. The commitment of this teacher has inspired many to be purposeful each day of life.

One way to invest in others is to mentor or adopt five or six people and intentionally spend time with them and pour into them. It may be grandkids, colleagues, schoolmates, or people who aren't Christian. Invest in them by praying for them every day.

John was passionate about Jesus and shared a powerful message. John had a clear sense of the message God had given him to share: Jesus is the only way, our only hope, and there is power in His name. Jesus is the answer to every problem we face. He said, "I am the way and the truth and the life. No one comes to the Father except through me" (John 14:6). Jesus wants us to evangelize others—to tell everyone about Him and see people become passionate believers. He wants us to live our lives with a purpose, sharing the powerful message that there's only one way to God: through His Son, through the love Jesus showed when He shed His blood on the cross at Calvary.

One of the greatest promises we have is the hope that comes in the name of the Lord. Jesus said, "You may ask me for anything in my name, and I will do it" (John 14:14).

Walking in John's Footsteps

We look up to people who are passionate about their beliefs. John shows us how to live as a passionate Christian. He assures us that once we have entered into a relationship with Jesus and accepted His gift of eternal life, nothing can take that away.

John lived his life with purpose as he served the believers in the early church. It's easy for us to follow the ways of the world around us and fall into the trap of taking more than giving. Jesus gives us an example of how to live a life of purpose when He said, "For even the Son of Man did not come to be served, but to serve" (Mark 10:45).

Sometimes we believe in God's ability to do big things but wonder if He'll do the small things for us. We doubt His power and this weakens the impact of the message we share with others. Once we grasp who God is and what Jesus did to give us a way to come to God, our message will have power.

I pray those who don't have a passion for Jesus Christ will acknowledge that He is the only way to God and will find answers, both for now and eternity. Once we receive the gift of His love, we claim His hope and promise of life with Him. I pray Christians who have not yet been baptized, who only go through the motions and attend church when convenient, will become serious about their faith. Be passionate for God!

WORKBOOK

Chapter Two Questions

Question: Describe something or someone that you are passionate about. How does thinking about this topic or person change your mindset and brighten your mood? Why do you have this passion? Has your passion rubbed off on anyone around you?

_____

_____

_____

_____

_____

_____

_____

_____

_____

_____

Question: Read and memorize 1 John 5:13. Do you have certainty that you are saved, or do you struggle with fears about losing your salvation? How does a belief in your eternal security give you a greater passion for Christ and for helping others know Him?

(If this is an area of particular struggle and doubt for you, reread the section in this chapter on eternal security and the verses listed. Consider talking with a mature believer who can help you in understanding the source of your doubts and fears and what the Bible says about eternal security.)

_____

_____

_____

_____

_____

_____

_____

_____

_____

_____

_____

Question: In whom are you intentionally investing, and how are you doing so? Can those around you, especially those whom you are serving, observe your passion for Jesus Christ? How is your passion impacting them personally or spiritually?

_____

_____

_____

_____

_____

_____

_____

_____

_____

_____

_____

Action: Study pure doctrine so you will have a passion for God's truth like John the Apostle. A book of systematic theology, a course on apologetics, or even a simple catechism can be vital to understanding what you believe and how it impacts your life. Ask your pastor or a Christian mentor for suggested resources.

Chapter Two Notes

_____

_____

_____

_____

_____

_____

_____

_____

_____

_____

_____

_____

_____

_____

_____

_____

_____

_____

_____

_____

_____

_____

_____

CHAPTER THREE

Barnabas—A Great Encourager

News of this reached the church in Jerusalem, and they sent Barnabas to Antioch. When he arrived and saw what the grace of God had done, he was glad and encouraged them all to remain true to the Lord with all their hearts. He was a good man, full of the Holy Spirit and faith, and a great number of people were brought to the Lord.

Then Barnabas went to Tarsus to look for Saul, and when he found him, he brought him to Antioch. So for a whole year Barnabas and Saul met with the church and taught great numbers of people. The disciples were called Christians first at Antioch.

During this time some prophets came down from Jerusalem to Antioch. One of them, named Agabus, stood up and through the Spirit predicted that a severe famine would spread over the entire Roman world. (This happened during the reign of Claudius.) The disciples, as each one was able, decided to provide help for the brothers and sisters living in Judea. This they did, sending their gift to the elders by Barnabas and Saul.

—Acts 11:22–30

As we consider the lives of people in the Bible, we're looking at ordinary giants. We learn from these examples how to keep God as the captain of our ship to steer a straight course and lead others to rest in Him. Many churches today are made up of similar giants of the faith— people who work behind the scenes. Every church has a handful of people who are visible and receive the praise of others, while others may work heartily behind the scenes. Sometimes, preachers, authors, and other people in prominent positions get recognition for their work. That goes with the territory. But often, the people behind the scenes make a huge difference.

Lessons from Barnabas

Barnabas didn't write any books in the New Testament, but he had a tremendous influence on the history of Christianity. It's important to remember that God sees our effort even when other people don't recognize it, which is what we find in the story of Barnabas.

Barnabas was the great encourager. He was a church leader who didn't have the prominence of Paul or John, but still had measurable impact on the kingdom. He worked in difficult situations and had to make hard decisions, but he made them with love, kindness, and a desire to please Jesus Christ. People sent their money with him because he was trustworthy. Barnabas kept plugging away, working in the church (Acts 11:30). Scripture notes, "He was a good man, full of the Holy Spirit and faith" (Acts 11:24). He was amazing!

I've met some great men and women throughout my

ministry—world-class Christians—who have never been recognized. Don't get discouraged! We may never be recognized the way we deserve, but God sees and understands. Jesus reminds us, "Be careful not to practice your righteousness in front of others to be seen by them. If you do, you will have no reward from your Father in heaven. ... Then your Father, who sees what is done in secret, will reward you" (Matthew 6:1, 4b). Those who are getting the rewards may have gotten all the rewards they're going to get on earth—they may not get any more in heaven. Let God do the rewarding, and let us focus on the working. That's what Barnabas did.

Barnabas encourages us to trust wholly in Jesus. The church in Jerusalem heard about the growth of the church in Antioch and sent Barnabas. A good man of faith and full of the Holy Spirit, Barnabas "encouraged them all to remain true to the Lord with all their hearts" (Acts 11:23). We learn the disciples were first called *Christians* at Antioch (Acts 11:26)—because of this man's leadership.

The name *Barnaba*s means "son of encouragement" (Acts 4:36). An encourager gives courage, hope, and confidence to people. Barnabas did this by working alongside Paul, teaching the people and encouraging them in their faith. We know Paul and Barnabas brought a message of hope because we read that "a great number of people were brought to the Lord" (Acts 11:24).

People who encourage others and bring them hope don't dwell on the past or put others down. They don't use negative language to admonish others while elevating their own biblical knowledge. An encourager tells people the good news that Jesus Christ is the one and only God who came to earth and walked among us and died on the cross to save the world. This type of ordinary giant reminds people of the hope and confidence we have in Christ: all who believe are part of God's family (Ephesians 2:19–22).

As an encourager, we can suppose Barnabas was upbeat and confident about God and in his work with the early church. We could use a lot more of that in this world. Be upbeat! Sure, the devil is strong, but Jesus is stronger. When you have Jesus, the devil has to go. When Jesus Christ is your Savior, the devil isn't strong enough for the power of Jesus' blood.

Once you've got Jesus, you've got everything. We all have issues, but in Jesus Christ we have someone who will never leave us or forsake us (Deuteronomy 31:8; Matthew 28:20), and we have the Holy Spirit living inside us (1 Corinthians 6:19). The Word of God will help guide us (Psalm 119:105), and heaven is our ultimate destination (Philippians 3:20). Friends, we have it all.

Barnabas encourages us to have faith in God. Barnabas demonstrated his faith in a way people could see. The Bible says, "He was a good man, full of the Holy Spirit and faith" (Acts 11:24). When people look at us, do they see a person of faith? We might be known as any number of great things, such as a great mom, a great businessperson, or a great community leader. But do people see us as a great person of faith?

What is faith? It's intangible; it's "confidence in what we hope for and assurance about what we do not see" (Hebrews 11:1). I like to use the acrostic FAITH: Forsaking All, I Trust Him. Barnabas put his faith in Jesus Christ, and it was evident to all.

When we're around someone like Barnabas, we can sense it. We know we're in the presence of someone special. We read in Acts that Barnabas spent quite a bit of time traveling with Paul (Acts 9, 11–15). How can we be like Barnabas? This doesn't automatically happen when we walk into church. It doesn't necessarily happen when we open our Bible. It takes spending time with God. This week I spent some time in the first pew of our church praying over the sanctuary and the upcoming service. There was a specific request I prayed for at about 8:30 a.m. Before I got up out of the pew that morning, God answered it. Isn't it amazing how He does that? He reaffirmed my faith.

Barnabas encourages us to be concerned about people's souls. We read in the passage that "for a whole year Barnabas and Saul met with the church and taught great numbers of people" (Acts 11:26) and "a great number of people were brought to the Lord" (Acts 11:24). Barnabas and Paul (previously known as Saul), were concerned about others' souls. It would be awesome if people could say that about us. Though we have legitimate concerns about relationships, financial situations, or health, our greatest concern should be people's souls! Where will they spend eternity? How are they living for Christ here? Only God can determine who is a saved soul and who isn't. That's not our job; it's between each individual person and God. Each of us is supposed to spread the good news by telling others about God's love, grace, and mercy, as Barnabas did.

Barnabas encourages us to be humble. We know Barnabas shows us how to be humble by what Scripture *doesn't* say. Paul defines godly humility in his letter to the Philippians, "Do nothing out of selfish ambition or vain conceit. Rather, in humility value others above yourselves" (Philippians 2:3). Scripture doesn't record any speeches or direct teaching of Barnabas, but it does record the meaning of his name.

We read in Acts that after Paul's conversion, "Barnabas took him and brought him to the apostles. He told them how Saul had seen the Lord and that the Lord had spoken to him and how in Damascus he had preached fearlessly in the name of Jesus" (Acts 9:27). In this passage, we see Barnabas lifting up Paul. In subsequent chapters, Barnabas and Paul traveled many miles together.

In his book, *Humility: The Beauty of Holiness*, Andrew Murray sheds light on how Barnabas is an example of a humble giant of the faith: "Unless pride dies in you, nothing of heaven can live in you."[5] Barnabas shed pride in his life so he could be "full of the Holy Spirit and faith" (Acts 11:24).

There are so many ways we allow pride to build up in our hearts. If we're going to have a demonstrable faith, a faith that walks in the Spirit, pride has to take a back seat or leave altogether. Like Barnabas, we have to not judge others and be a witness for Jesus Christ.

Walking in Barnabas' Footsteps

We can choose to be like Barnabas, a son of encouragement, a person who shows others hope and confidence in God. Jesus Christ is the greatest, our Savior, and He changes our lives and gives us a positive outlook. We need to demonstrate our faith in such a way people can feel and sense it. We do this by caring about their souls because that's the only thing that matters in the end. Walk in the Spirit and grow in your faith.

We've received valuable coaching tips from Paul about how to start growing into a giant of the faith. John's story shows us ordinary giants have extraordinary passion about God. Barnabas encourages us to continue to grow in our faith so we can share it with others. All of these concepts provide steps we can take to stay on course and become an ordinary giant for God.

WORKBOOK

Chapter Three Questions

Question: Describe a believer who has influenced and encouraged you, though they are not famous or recognized. When have you been used by God in a behind-the-scenes role?

_____

_____

_____

_____

_____

_____

_____

_____

_____

Question: What are some specific areas and ways that people—including believers—need hope? And what are some specific ways that you can offer them hope rooted in Jesus Christ (rather than mere positive thinking)?

_____

_____

_____

_____

_____

_____

_____

_____

_____

_____

_____

Question: Who are some people whose souls you are concerned about? List them and commit to pray for them daily. Ask God to give you an opportunity with each one to address the real issue in their lives—their relationship with Jesus Christ. Be sure to present truth in a humble, encouraging manner like Barnabas, and let God do His work.

_____

_____

_____

_____

_____

_____

_____

_____

_____

_____

_____

_____

Action: Study more about the life of Barnabas. How did God specifically use him to launch the ministries of both Paul and John Mark? How did Barnabas' belief in and encouragement of these two men—whom others did not always trust—eventually pay off for God's kingdom? Then read about the life of a famous evangelist, such as Billy Graham or D. L. Moody. Look for ways God used ordinary, unrecognized encouragers to help launch and sustain their ministries?

Chapter Three Notes

_____

_____

_____

_____

_____

_____

_____

_____

_____

_____

_____

_____

_____

_____

_____

_____

_____

_____

_____

_____

_____

_____

CHAPTER FOUR

James—The Practical Christian

My dear brothers and sisters, take note of this: Everyone should be quick to listen, slow to speak and slow to become angry, because human anger does not produce the righteousness that God desires. Therefore, get rid of all moral filth and the evil that is so prevalent and humbly accept the word planted in you, which can save you.
—James 1:19–27

Sam hung back from the crowd gathered in the church entryway. What if he wasn't dressed right? What if he said or did the wrong thing? Was he supposed to raise his hands during the service? It's easy for new Christ-followers to feel overwhelmed with the sense there are invisible rules they're expected to know and follow. They're happy to be in Jesus' lifeboat, but they have no idea if they might do or say something that will sink the ship—or at the very least, rock the boat.

They understand they have made a choice to follow Christ, but they're not quite sure what it looks like to look to God as their captain and leader. We can fill that role in their lives by showing them practical ways to live for and with Jesus. And new Christians and mature Christians alike can look to James as an example of an ordinary giant who gave his life for God.

Lessons from James

The Bible mentions more than one person named James. Two of Jesus' disciples were named James— James son of Alphaeus and James the son of Zebedee. Jesus' half-brother was also named James; scholars believe this is the person who wrote the letter to "the twelve tribes scattered among the nations" (James 1:1). James, the half-brother of Jesus, served as the pastor, or co-pastor, of the church of Jerusalem, which was the first church of Christ followers.[6]

Before James, the half-brother of Jesus, arrived at the place in his life where he lead the church in Jerusalem or wrote a letter to Jewish Christians, he did a complete about-face in his thinking. He went from thinking Jesus was crazy (Mark 3:21) and not believing in Him (John 7:5) to gathering in the upper room with Jesus' followers after His death and resurrection (Acts 1:14). Paul says Jesus appeared to James after His resurrection (1 Corinthians 15:7), which may have been the defining moment that turned James to faith.

James had a practical faith. He knew living for Christ wasn't complicated. Once we trust in Jesus as Savior, He takes over the front seat of our lives. Perhaps you've seen those bumper stickers that say, "God is my co-pilot." Let me change that to: "God is my captain." In this book, we've used the analogy of a ship's captain. God, as our captain, is the one who steers our ship. He gives us a guide to live by, a church to encourage and strengthen us, and fellowship with other believers. He gives us the Holy Spirit to convict us when we're doing things we shouldn't be doing, and He gives us a heavenly home when this life is over.

We've made Christianity a lot more difficult than it's meant to be with rules and regulations. We think of pastors as those who judge how well we're living the Christian life. But they're not our judge. They're in the same boat with us. John reminds us there's only one judge, the Holy Spirit: "When he comes, he will convict the world concerning sin and righteousness and judgment" (John 16:8 ESV).

In his letter, James gives a practical dissertation on living an upright and moral life. He writes, "But whoever looks intently into the perfect law that gives freedom, and continues in it—not forgetting what they have heard, but doing it—they will be blessed in what they do" (James 1:25). This is the simplicity I was talking about—receive it, walk in it, and live by it.

James encourages us to look into the Word of God and do what it says.

Anyone who listens to the word but does not do what it says is like someone who looks at his face in a mirror and, after looking at himself, goes away and immediately forgets what he looks like.
—James 1:23–24

No debate, no questioning. James gives practical suggestions for Christian living. One such suggestion is to stop gossiping and talking about other people. We each have two ears and one mouth—God's trying to get our attention. He wants us to listen twice as much as we talk. We've already learned from Barnabas that a key step to becoming a leader for Jesus, a gentle giant, is to encourage others instead of putting them down.

It's not hard to be a Christian. Once we ask Jesus Christ to come into our lives, life takes on a whole different meaning. There are no rules to follow; we now follow a person and allow Him to guide us through life. He will lead and direct our paths and show us the way to go (Proverbs 3:5–6). James reinforces the practical nature of Christianity throughout his book.

James had a practical conversion. James was converted by believing in Jesus' resurrection. He was a *show-me* convert. Despite growing up with Jesus, he didn't become a Christian until Jesus was raised to life as He promised. Until Jesus walked out of the tomb, James didn't believe. A lot of people I know are show-me people who won't believe until they see something happen.

People today want proof something is worth the investment. They might say, "I know you go to church, but is Jesus who He said He was?" We live in the twenty-first century, where one acceptable mantra is, "Let's eat, drink, and be merry, for tomorrow we die—why should we worry about religion?" Becoming a Christian is not only the most logical thing a person can do—it's the greatest thing a person can do!

Pastor and author Andy Stanley makes an interesting

connection between our own mortality and Jesus' resurrection. He said, "If a man can predict his own death and resurrection, and pull it off ... I go with whatever that man says."[7] If someone can predict his death and be raised back to life, that man is God and His name is Jesus Christ. He's the person we need to follow. Do we follow all these Hollywood starlets and leading men who will disappoint us? They're not God. If we follow the way they live, we're going to wind up with a short life.

When James saw that Jesus did exactly what He said He would, he realized, "He may be my brother, but he's more than my brother. That man is God and I'm going to follow Him." James became an amazing convert and a leader in the church at Jerusalem. Historians say when they found James upon his death, his knees were so calloused from the time he spent praying for the needs of others, people realized he was a true prayer warrior.[8]

Once we become a Christian, our life will never be the same. We accept Jesus as God, we receive the Word of God and the Holy Spirit, and we decide to start living for Him. But Satan wants to come in and change our thinking. He tempts Christians to forsake our beliefs and rely on feelings and emotions, forgetting the truth of Scripture. Church is important in resisting such temptation because it helps us focus every single week on doing the right thing. Prayer, Bible study, worship, and fellowship are all important. It's not complicated; we've made it complicated.

James had a practical, simple faith. The faith James had was simple and practical, but most importantly, it was genuine. We can't do any work for God if we don't have faith. In his letter to the Romans, Paul tells us that the first step in working for God is making our faith real. "Everyone who calls on the name of the Lord will be saved" (Romans 10:13). God knows our hearts. The first step is to call upon Him for salvation.

The second step is to listen to God's Word. James, a practical Christian, reminds us: "Do not merely listen to the word, and so deceive yourselves. Do what it says" (James 1:22). Jesus also teaches us that many things can snatch away the seed of the Word: the devil, the world, troubles, worries, persecution, or trials (Matthew 13:19–22; Mark 4:15–19; Luke 8:12–14). James leads us with heartfelt guidance. Don't be confused by the world or caught off guard by your own evil desires (James 1:14). Sometimes, it's a ploy by the evil one, but God is stronger.

As a teenager, I gave my life to Christ to become a minister. My life could have gone numerous directions. Remaining focused was the hardest thing about being a Christian in my twenties. It's easy for people to go in different directions. I see this happening in the church today. We listen to other voices in the world. The fact that I'm still ministering helps me realize how strong God is. I believe and trust, and part of that is believing and acting on the power of prayer.

This leads us to the third step in developing genuine faith. James says, "Blessed is the one who perseveres under trial because, having stood the test, that person will receive the crown of life that the Lord has promised to those who love him" (James 1:12).

John MacArthur, a great preacher from California, said, "The true gospel is a call to self-denial. It is not a call to self-fulfillment."[9] When we become a believer, this simple faith puts God in the captain's chair. We deny what we want to do and decide to ask God what He wants. It's not about getting our way all the time and praying blessings for ourselves. It's about praying to extend the kingdom.

The wisest man who ever lived, King Solomon, wrote, "Trust in the LORD with all your heart and lean not on your own understanding; in all your ways submit to Him, and He will make your paths straight" (Proverbs 3:5–6). Listen and obey. What does God want? This is a simple faith. It's about believing and doing. The doing part is key, and a response of obedience to God. He's watching what's going on in our lives.

As Christians, we should make an effort to pray daily, read our Bible, attend worship regularly, tithe on our income, and be a witness with word and action. Once we choose to live by the precepts of the Word of God, it's not complicated. Consistent obedience to God's Word and His commands develops a pattern of Christian living.

What are we doing for God? When was the last time we invited someone to come to church with us? When was the last time we prayed God would use us in an extraordinary way? When was the last time we prayed for the sick and hurting? When was the last time we took a dinner to someone in need—without fanfare? Or helped a homeless person? Or mentored a child at school? When was the last time we did things that were not self-fulfilling but selfless?

James lived out his faith in practical ways. God speaks through James to say that our words matter. People matter.

Actions matter. What we say is important. What we do with our hands can have both positive and negative impacts. We might use our hands to build beautiful cathedrals or to take, hurt, and steal. Our feet—we need to careful where we go. God says our feet are blessed when they go to present the gospel (Romans 10:15), but they can also take us places we ought to avoid. Our eyes can show us paths or directions we need to travel, but we also use our eyes to see things that are not pleasing to God.

James knew actions, including our speech, matter. The example he gives in the first chapter of his letter concerns our words: "Those who consider themselves religious and yet do not keep a tight rein on their tongues deceive themselves, and their religion is worthless" (James 1:26). Swearing matters. When we use curse words, they matter. All of us—kids, teenagers, and adults—need to guard our mouths. If we claim to be Christians, we should watch what we saying and what we post. Using profanity in speech or online is something we can't take back.

During a children's talk, I once gave all the kids tubes of toothpaste and instructed them to squeeze until empty and then to put it all back in the tube. They looked at me and said, "You can't, it's already out." The same thing is true of the words we say about people, and of profanity, lies, insinuations, gossip, or statements we'll regret later. We can't put them back where they came from.

In the book *Experiencing God,* Henry Blackaby said, "God is interested in developing your character. At times He lets you proceed in your disobedience, but He will never let you go too far without discipline to bring you back."[10] When we make a wrong decision, the Holy Spirits helps us recognize it's not God's will and guides us back to the right path. Aren't you glad God is our heavenly Father? When we go down a wrong path, He doesn't kick us out of the family. He brings us gently back in where we ought to be.

The question we need to ask ourselves is, "Are we part of the family?" This is where casual Christianity has its biggest problem. Being baptized, tithing on your income, being solemn or raising hands during worship, doesn't make anyone a Christian. Realizing we have sinned, asking Jesus to be our Lord and Savior and to take away our sins, makes us a Christian. Jesus becomes our Savior. "Everyone who calls on the name of the Lord will be saved" (Romans 10:13). Once we do, then naturally we want to join the church, be baptized, give our tithes, and share our faith. But if we haven't called on His name for salvation, everything in Christianity seems foreign.

There are a lot of church members who have never been born again. For those people, Christianity seems complicated, prayer seems foreign, Bible reading is a chore, and going to church every week is difficult. As Christians, we grow closer to the Lord when we read and meditate on the Word of God, pray, worship, and give. This is what a Christian does. We watch what we say and where we go and what we do, hear, and see. It's not complicated.

James was a very practical Christian. I'm convinced churches of all denominations would be full every week if we lived out our Christian faith and weren't hypocritical, instead loving and serving. It should come naturally.

I remember a revival that took place during my childhood. I was about eight or nine years old. At the end of the service, the preacher asked everyone to take some handbills advertising the revival and distribute them. I took a stack of handbills and put them on cars in the parking lot of the church. I didn't know he meant to give them to people who weren't already at church! I just followed his directions to the best of my ability. It's the same for Christians. It's not difficult: God wants us to have—and exercise—simple faith.

Walking in James' Footsteps

James was a show-me convert; nothing could change his mind once he received Christ. How can we be more like James? Once we become followers of Christ, know Him, and experience the forgiveness of our sins, that should be all we need. We make this too hard. It's about praying, reading the Bible, and loving others. It's about coming to church and being with one another. Why are we making it so complicated?

If we hang around people who make sinful life choices, they're going to bring us down. If we read trash, we start to think bad thoughts. If we skip church one week, it's easier the second week—and the third. Before we know it, we're like the world, with church not part of our regular routine.

Satan is trying to bring down the church, and he wants to bring us down individually. We know what's right and wrong because the Bible instructs us. James reminds us,

"Do not merely listen to the word, and so deceive yourselves. Do what it says" (James 1:22). Be a practical Christian. We don't need a book to tell us how to do it—what we need is an open heart and an open mind.

We need more ordinary giants who will show others how to have simple, practical faith, as James did. We can lead others to Christ by example as we take steps to develop our own genuine faith: call on the Lord for salvation, listen to God's Word and do what it says, persevere under trial, and live the way God wants us to live.

Maybe our children, or others in our circles of influence, need us to be more practical James lived out his faith in practical ways because he understood that actions matter. We can show simple, practical faith in the way we live everyday life.

WORKBOOK

Chapter Four Questions

Question: In what ways does Christianity sometimes seem complicated to you? In what ways has the modern church complicated it? How does having God as your captain clarify and simplify the Christian life?

_____

_____

_____

_____

_____

_____

_____

_____

_____

Question: What objections and doubts almost kept you from Christ? How did God show His power to you? How would you talk to someone else who had similar doubts and help them to see the reality of who Christ is?

_____

_____

_____

_____

_____

_____

_____

_____

_____

_____

_____

_____

Question: How does a life built on reading, studying, and obeying God's Word help to keep your Christianity focused and genuine? What practical actions does the Word instruct you to do as a Christ-follower? How can you move from daily reading to consistent application of the Bible?

_____

_____

_____

_____

_____

_____

_____

_____

_____

_____

_____

_____

Action: Read the book of James and do an in-depth study of this practical book through a commentary or a Bible study. Choose one passage that you need to apply and memorize those verses.

Chapter Four Notes

_____

_____

_____

_____

_____

_____

_____

_____

_____

_____

_____

_____

_____

_____

_____

_____

_____

_____

_____

_____

_____

_____

_____

CHAPTER FIVE

Luke—A Gifted Person

Many have undertaken to draw up an account of the things that have been fulfilled[a] among us, just as they were handed down to us by those who from the first were eye-witnesses and servants of the word. With this in mind, since I myself have carefully investigated everything from the beginning, I too decided to write an orderly account for you, most excellent Theophilus, so that you may know the certainty of the things you have been taught.

—Luke 1:1–4

In the last twenty or thirty years, some people have got-ten the notion that to be a Christian is to be soft intellectually. They think Christians don't always experi-ence the rigors of a sound education. Some of the greatest minds, however, have been Christ-followers. Augustine of Hippo, for example, was one of the brightest, sharpest men of his time. He was notorious across his region as a rich socialite, but then he encountered Jesus and gave his life to Christ. He became known as Saint Augustine, an intellectual giant. Sir Isaac Newton, a master mathematician and brilliant thinker who wrote about opaqueness and light, is another example of a Christian intellect.

Time Magazine noted outstanding Christian leaders who lived closer to our time than Saint Augustine and Newton. For their contributions to society, the magazine featured C. S. Lewis in 1947[11] and Reinhold Niebuhr in 1948.[12] Both men were Christians with amazing intellectual capacities. In fact, nearly two-thirds of all scientific Nobel prize winners have claimed to be Christians.[13]

Lessons from Luke

We also find examples of *intellectual giants* in God's Word. Luke was a man who had tremendous intellect and influence; he wrote the Gospel of Luke as well as the Book of Acts, which tells the story of the early church. Luke was a physician and a Gentile—a non-Jew—yet God used him in a special way.

Luke used his gifts to glorify God. God often attracts the brightest minds of the time. Born in Antioch, a physician by profession, Luke became a disciple of Paul and followed him until his martyrdom. He served the Lord, alongside Paul, and used his education to advance the kingdom. Trained intellectually, he used his gifts for the glory of God.[14]

As a physician, Luke understood the way things fit together. As an intellectual, he wanted to "sort the truth and report the facts."[15] In his account for Theophilus, Luke says, "I myself have carefully investigated everything from the beginning ... to write an orderly account for you"

(Luke 1:3). He understood the Scriptures and saw how God orchestrated life here on earth so masterfully. He wanted to follow the One who can do that, so he came to Jesus Christ.

In my graduating class, we had several would-be physicians. I'll never forget when I was dealing with cancer twenty years ago, one of them kept calling to check on me. He said, "Every day when I see my patients, there's one or two I pray with because I want them to know I'm a physician, but I'm a Christian first."

Luke used his profession for the glory of God. Christians occupy a wide variety of professions both inside the church and in the secular world. We find Christians who are doctors, lawyers, mill workers, retail clerks, or servers at a drive-through window. Any profession can be evangelistic! Instead of saying, "Have a good day" while handing out food, we can say, "God bless you" and watch the response. God wants us to use the platform He has given us no matter where we may work or serve.

Some people trip over stumbling blocks over minor issues, which can be detrimental to the church. Once Jesus saves us, we are brothers and sisters in Christ forever. That's a big, important thing to remember. Jesus' words in John 3:16 have enough gospel in one verse to save the entire world! All who believe and understand who Jesus is and all who ask Jesus to come into their heart are saved by God's grace. It's not about denominational labels or what kind of music you like. It's not whether you wear a tie or jeans or which translation of the Bible you use. We need to set aside our preferential beliefs and focus on winning people for Jesus Christ. Let's use our professions and platforms to glorify Him!

Many businesspeople have followed Luke's example of using their professions for the glory of God. J. C. Penney was a devout Christian who based his life and business on the faith and Christian principles he learned as a child and rediscovered as an adult.[16]

Don't tell me Christians can't be winners! One of the coaches with the most wins in NCAA basketball history, John Wooden, was a devout Christian.[17]

Joe Gibbs, NFL Hall of Fame coach, loves God, has a deep relationship with Him, and has learned to trust the Lord in times of adversity.[18] Don't tell me tough guys can't be Christians.

Clayton Kershaw of the Los Angles Dodgers is a fellow believer who consistently shares his faith in Jesus from the platform he has been given. Additionally, he and his wife Ellen have funded missionary projects in Zambia to protect the most vulnerable in our world. A giant, indeed!

Luke used his gifts to reach others for Christ. Doctor Luke used his "skill [as] a surgeon to [probe] for truth."[19] He wanted Theophilus to "know the certainty of the things you have been taught" (Luke 1:4), to know and understand the truth about Jesus. He addresses Theophilus as a man of prominence to encourage him to draw even closer to God.[20]

We need to follow Luke's example of being a leader for Christ and embrace all our outreach opportunities. Luke used his position as an intellectual to do this by talking with eyewitnesses to write an account for Theophilus (Luke 1:2–3). He compiled an accurate history of Jesus' ministry and the history of the early church to reach those who might not have been reached in other ways. The late, great Presbyterian minister D. James Kennedy said, "Christ, who came meek and mild to save us from pain and suffering, was the One who talked more about hell than any other person in Scripture."[21] He also said, "You cannot say, 'No, Lord,' and mean both words; one annuls the other. If you say no to Him, then He is not your Lord."[22]

The Lord gives us many opportunities to be used for His glory. We can use our mouths to praise God, our hands and feet to serve Him, and our minds to help make the world a place that glorifies its' Creator. Don't fall into the trap of engaging with everything that comes across the Internet. We don't have to comment on everything or be an expert on everything. We can put our efforts into keeping our platform strong for Jesus. Our lives aren't about us or how much stuff we accumulate or how great we are. We are to be conduits to reach others for Christ.

Rick Warren said, "What you do with the influence you currently have will determine whether or not your influence grows more."[23] If we want to have a greater ministry and influence more people for Christ, it starts with being faithful where we are. God will provide us with opportunities to serve.

Luke used his gifts to help other people. As with other ordinary giants we've observed, Luke was so busy serving and helping we don't find much mention of him in the New Testament. He's mentioned by name only three times, each at the end of three of Paul's letters, to send greetings to fellow Christians and to reassure them that

Luke was with Paul and caring for him (Colossians 4:14; 2 Timothy 4:11; Philemon 1:24).

In current times, using your gifts to help others may look like Melissa—the business manager of a Christian organization—who thrives on numbers and details. She is the go-to person whenever anyone has questions. When the organization sponsors events that minister and benefit its members and guests, Melissa works behind the scenes to make sure things run smoothly. She has others to help, and together they use their gifts to help others succeed in *their* God-given work and ministry.

Walking in Luke's Footsteps

Luke leads by example in his life and writing. We've observed how he served others to advance God's kingdom. He used his gifts to glorify God, reach others for Christ, and help other people. Above all, Luke wanted to help Theophilus—and others—come to know Jesus better, and he wanted to help his friends, including Paul.

Jesus has always attracted those with bright minds, and He still does. If you are curious about Christianity, go back and look at history. Examine some of the brightest people who have been attracted to Jesus—people we look up to as intellectual giants When we encounter the truth about Jesus, the greatest truth given to people, that truth will set us free (John 8:32). Once we understand who Jesus is, we realize He's the King of kings and Lord of lords, the One who makes it all fit together perfectly. We glorify God when we help others see Him clearly and draw near to Him. Whatever God has given us in the way of platform or profession, whatever we've been blessed to accomplish, we need to use it for the glory of God.

Our involvement in church is one way we can reach others for Christ. Gary was the head usher for our church when I arrived. The thing I loved most about Gary was how he introduced himself when people walked in the door for the first time. They would tell him their names, and he never failed to remember each one. The next time they met, he would remember their names, both first and last. At his funeral recently someone said, "I had been visiting churches in the area and wasn't sure where I would join. I visited here one time and then returned a couple of months later. I walked in the front door and Gary remembered my first and last name. I knew I'd found the right place. There was someone here who cared about me." Gary had a gift for reaching out to others. He used his gift in service to God to show others God cares for them.

Luke's life and writing indicate he was deeply devoted to Jesus. He wasn't afraid to use his intellectual abilities, his professional platform, and his influence to point others to Jesus. This ordinary giant's example calls us to examine our own pattern of living. God is our captain, but He wants to use our ship and its abilities to lead others to shore.

What are we doing for God? What will we leave as a legacy? Will anyone stand up and say, "He led me to Christ"? "She helped me know Him better"? "This person taught my Sunday school class, served as a deacon in my church, or shared the gospel as a missionary in my community"?

WORKBOOK

Chapter Five Questions

Question: What are some ways that an intellectually-gifted person could be of great service in God's kingdom? What are some particular dangers that an intellectual Christian might face (1 Corinthians 1:26–31, 8:1; James 3:1)?

_____

_____

_____

_____

_____

_____

_____

_____

_____

_____

Question: What particular gifts and skills has God given you? What is your profession? How can you use each of these things for God's glory and the building up of His kingdom? Give some examples of people in all walks of life who have used their platforms to honor Jesus and point others to Him.

_____

_____

_____

_____

_____

_____

_____

_____

_____

_____

_____

_____

Question: How are you prioritizing God's will and others' needs over your own comfort or interests? How are you being faithful with the opportunities and influence God has given you right now?

_____

_____

_____

_____

_____

_____

_____

_____

_____

_____

_____

_____

_____

Action: Write out a list of your talents, skills, and opportunities. Next to each, write a way that you can use that gift to glorify God and help others.

Chapter Five Notes

CHAPTER SIX

Matthew—The Unpopular One

As Jesus went on from there, he saw a man named Matthew sitting at the tax collector's booth. "Follow me," he told him, and Matthew got up and followed him.

While Jesus was having dinner at Matthew's house, many tax collectors and sinners came and ate with him and his disciples. When the Pharisees saw this, they asked his disciples, "Why does your teacher eat with tax collectors and sinners?"

On hearing this, Jesus said, "It is not the healthy who need a doctor, but the sick. But go and learn what this means: 'I desire mercy, not sacrifice.' For I have not come to call the righteous, but sinners."

—Matthew 9:9–13

Chad struggles to accept God would really love him and help him steer a straight course in his life. He hesitates to attend church because he doesn't want to get close to other people. He believes he can barely take care of himself, let alone have anything left to offer others. Chad is certain everyone at his local church knows and remembers his past, when he had to flee bad choices and circumstances. However, what faith he does have spills over at work, in the care, patience, and love he gives his special education students. It affects how he interacts with family, as he takes care of his parents. Chad feels he doesn't fit in at church, yet Jesus is transforming his life in other ways.

Lessons from Matthew

We don't think of those with undesirable pasts as giants or leaders for God. Matthew, one of Jesus' disciples, had an interesting background; he was a tax collector (Matthew 9:9). In New Testament times, tax collectors had a lot of street savvy. They achieved their positions by figuratively buying their way in. They collected taxes for Rome, which was in charge of most of the world. To pay for roads, exotic amphitheaters, and other buildings across the empire, Rome collected taxes from everyone.[24]

The tax collectors were hated by all, but they had the backing of the Roman army. Matthew would have brought a few soldiers with him when he told a householder, "You owe this amount of money." Anyone who tried to resist paying the tax bill could be thrown in jail. The people hated tax collectors. Matthew was such a person.

As Jesus went on from there, he saw a man named Matthew sitting at the tax collector's booth. "Follow me," He told him, and Matthew got up and followed Him.
—Matthew 9:9

Jesus had a way of connecting with all people, including the lost. It's important for Christians not to barricade themselves in with other Christians in their realm of influence. Sometimes as Christians, we associate only with other believers. We need to step outside our spheres of influence and connect with others! After Jesus' death, resurrection, and ascension back to heaven, we read:

> *Then the apostles returned to Jerusalem from the hill called the Mount of Olives, a Sabbath day's walk from the city. When they arrived, they went upstairs to the room where they were staying. Those present were Peter, John, James and Andrew; Philip and Thomas, Bartholomew and Matthew; James son of Alphaeus and Simon the Zealot, and Judas son of James.*
> *—Acts 1:12–13*

We see Matthew listed here as one of Jesus' disciples, an ordinary giant called by Jesus to share the good news of the gospel. Matthew was there at the ascension and in the upper room. Jesus loved Matthew. Why should we consider him a true spiritual giant?

Matthew was unpopular, but Jesus accepted him. Jesus doesn't care about our history; He accepted Matthew just as he was. I hear people say, "I would love to be a Christian, but I'm not good enough to go to church. I've done so many bad things, God would never accept me." The good news is, God still forgives! Whatever our background, God forgives us if we ask Him. But we have to ask. Jesus does the saving. People don't need to clean up to come to Jesus. We must remember this important lesson. Jesus set the example—we should invite people to come as they are.

Renowned evangelist Billy Graham said, "The people who followed Him were unique in their generation. They turned their world upside down because their hearts had been turned right side up. The world has never been the same."[25]

Our hearts are the problem. God wants to change our hearts of stone into hearts that are forgiven (Ezekiel 36:26). He wants to make us alive to serve Him. Our God is a good God. He took someone like Matthew, a sinner, and changed him and invited him to be one of the twelve disciples. Think about it: Matthew was someone God used to help change the world, yet the people around him thought he was terrible. God can use anyone!

Each of us can think of people we've met or read about who were going down the wrong road until Jesus came into their lives. They realized Jesus is the Son of God and that He died on the cross for the sins of all, so that they, and all of us, can receive His grace and forgiveness and become transformed. That's what happened to Matthew.

Matthew was unpopular, but he found new life and purpose in following Christ. Matthew discovered Jesus was the only one who could give new life and purpose. His old way of living made people miserable, as he stole and made life wretched for many. When Matthew started following Jesus, he had a new purpose and a plan that God gave him, and his life was never the same. He followed Jesus all the way to Calvary's cross and beyond. God used Matthew, and He can use every one of us.

Rick Warren said, "What gives me the most hope every day is God's grace; knowing that his grace is going to give me the strength for whatever I face, knowing that nothing is a surprise to God."[26]

Once we become a Christian, Jesus begins to guide our paths. We have decisions to make; why would we make them without asking God for His wisdom? King Solomon tells us how to do this: "Trust in the LORD with all your heart and lean not on your own understanding; in all your ways submit to Him and He will make your paths straight" (Proverbs 3:5–6).

As Christians, we follow Jesus. It's that simple. We stop making our own decisions; everything about us now belongs to God. I read a wonderful article on Crosswalk about how Christians can grow in their faith:[27]

1. Be willing to drop everything for Jesus, as Matthew did.

2. Rethink how we use our money. Most people I know are in bondage to their money. They think it's theirs—they don't realize it's God's. When we become liberators, helping other people along the way, it will change how we look at money.

3. Recognize sacrifice and appreciate it. Matthew appreciated what God was calling him to do. There will be some sacrifices as we learn and grow in our faith. God may ask us to do things we're not comfortable with. I remember training our deacons, and about half of them said the same thing: "I feel uncomfortable going to the hospital." Yet, their apprehension hasn't stopped even one of them from going; they go

and they do it well. Why? They're willing to
sacrifice for God.

4. Don't hesitate, not even for a moment. When
   God calls you to do something, do it.

5. To grow in your faith, care deeply about the im-
   poverished and the unreached. Never be
   satisfied; always try to win more people to
   Christ. Care about those who are hungry—
   physically and spiritually.

*Matthew was unpopular, but he started working for Je-
sus immediately.* Matthew didn't waste time but
immediately went to work for Jesus. God calls all of us to
work for Him now. If we wait until we're ready, we will
never work effectively for God. He isn't looking for our
ability, but our availability. We had a couple of guys in
our church volunteer for a recent mission trip. One young
man, Ryan, has cancer, and the other volunteer was
ninety-years old.

When Ryan came home and joined the church, he
asked straightaway, "How can I serve?" I said, "You're
pretty good at archery, aren't you? Why don't you start a
program for the kids?" So he did. That's what needs to
happen; whatever you're good at, go do. Those who can
teach, teach. Those who can sing, sing. Whatever your
gifts, use them for His glory (Romans 12:3–8).

Walking in Matthew's Footsteps

It doesn't matter how popular we are, we can follow in this ordinary giant's footsteps and live productive lives for Jesus. In spite of his past, Matthew understood Jesus accepted and called him. He found new life and purpose in following Christ, and he started working for Jesus immediately.

I'm convinced there are some Matthews reading this—those who don't feel qualified to be Christians. Yet, Jesus is saying, "Come, follow me" (Matthew 4:19). We think since we're unpopular, God won't want us either. We might think, *"Wait a minute, I need to take care of a few things first."* No, just follow! See what God will do.

D. L. Moody said, "A lighthouse does not have a drum beaten or a trumpet blown in order to proclaim the proximity of the lighthouse: it is its own witness. And so if we have the true light in us it will show itself."[28] We are to shine for God. And as our light shines before men, it will help those on troubled seas make it safely to shore.

WORKBOOK

Chapter Six Questions

Question: What sort of past do you tend to look at as disqualifying a person from being a leader for God? Are there issues in your own past that you try to hide or that you feel make you an inferior Christian? Are there people in your church whom you have judged or ostracized because of their lives before Christ (or mistakes they have made and repented of as a believer)?

_____

_____

_____

_____

_____

_____

_____

Question: Whose advice was Matthew following, and how did he make money decisions as a tax collector? How did this all change when he made the decision to follow Jesus? How do you know if you are making financial decisions based on godly wisdom or worldly wisdom? What are some examples from your life of each type of decision?

_____

_____

_____

_____

_____

_____

_____

_____

_____

_____

_____

_____

Question: The same attention to detail that made Matthew excel as a tax collector made him the most detailed of the gospel writers. What is an ability or gift that you used for selfish or hurtful means that you are now able to use for God's glory?

_____

_____

_____

_____

_____

_____

_____

_____

_____

_____

_____

Action: As Matthew did, come to God just as you are. Give your past sins and mistakes to Him and rejoice in the ways He is changing you. What is something outside your comfort zone that God is calling you to do for Him? Like Matthew, follow Jesus right away.

Chapter Six Notes

_____

_____

_____

_____

_____

_____

_____

_____

_____

_____

_____

_____

_____

_____

_____

_____

_____

_____

_____

_____

CHAPTER SEVEN

Thomas—The Discouraged Christian

Now Thomas (also known as Didymus), one of the Twelve, was not with the disciples when Jesus came. So the other disciples told him, "We have seen the Lord!"

But he said to them, "Unless I see the nail marks in his hands and put my finger where the nails were, and put my hand into his side, I will not believe."

A week later his disciples were in the house again, and Thomas was with them. Though the doors were locked, Jesus came and stood among them and said, "Peace be with you!" Then he said to Thomas, "Put your finger here; see my hands. Reach out your hand and put it into my side. Stop doubting and believe." Thomas said to him, "My Lord and my God!" Then Jesus told him, "Because you have seen me, you have believed; blessed are those who have not seen and yet have believed."

Jesus performed many other signs in the presence of his disciples, which are not recorded in this book. But these are written that you may believe that Jesus is the Messiah, the Son of God, and that by believing you may have life in his name.

—John 20:24–31

A friend and I were both called to ministry during the same timeframe. He was a gifted speaker, and when he spoke people were naturally drawn to him—he had a big personality. Things happened in his life that didn't go the way he wanted, and after a year or two, he left the ministry. We're still good friends today but despite all of his abilities, he gave it all away. Some of you have great abilities, but God's not looking for your talent. He's looking for your availability, your commitment, and your desire to follow Him.

Lessons from Thomas

Thomas was one of the twelve disciples. What's one word we always put in front of his name? "Doubting" Thomas. Everyone thinks he was a weak Christian. But John records a different side of Thomas, noting his passion for Christ: "Then Thomas (also known as Didymus) said to the rest of the disciples, 'Let us also go, that we may die with him'" (John 11:16).

Thomas was anything but a wallflower Christian. He was bold, a bit like Peter. When they thought Jesus might face death, Thomas was the only disciple who said, "Let's go with Him." This ordinary giant was passionate for Jesus. He gets a bad rap for his "doubting" statement, but let's unpack that in a bit.

Thomas had fire and passion. I've been pastoring for many years, and I can't tell you how many people have been saved by the glorious gospel of Jesus Christ. They start with a passion for God, witnessing to everyone they come in contact with. But it's often fellow Christians who put a damper on their boldness. Don't do that—let them be on fire.

Something happens, someone disappoints them, or they succumb to temptation and fall. Oftentimes, there is an intense sense of guilt that comes upon bold, passionate believers who stumble and fall. This is what happened to Thomas. He was as bold as you can get; then Jesus was put on trial and found guilty. Jesus' life ended in such a way that it took Thomas down. Jesus Christ was supposed to be the leader and save the world—when He died, Thomas' dreams died, too. A lot of Christians are passionate for God until something happens, and it sets them back. Next thing you know they're on the bench, won't come to church, and mad at the world.

Jesus knew that about Thomas' doubt and chose him anyway. In the focus passage, Thomas wasn't with the other disciples when Jesus came to them after the resurrection. He'd had enough and left his faithful group of disciples. But he came back.

Thomas grew discouraged, but Jesus called him anyway. Jesus selected Thomas knowing full well he would have doubts. He knew Thomas had strengths and weaknesses, the same as all of us. Yet, He calls us to do something for His glory. Each of us can do something for Christ, but more importantly, He can do something through us if we'll allow Him.

The trouble is we have perfection problems—we think unless we can be perfect and walk with Him every moment of every day, we can't live for Christ. Yet, we can! We can serve Christ right where we are. Granted, He never condones sin—He doesn't want us to live sinful lifestyles or choose to live in a sinful way. But if we fall into sin, into temptation, He's willing to forgive us (1 John 1:9), pick us up, and put us back on the pathway of service.

Thomas was an example of someone who was passionate for Christ. Let's go die for Him if we have to! This is the same guy who said, "No, I'm not going to believe anymore," like a lot of Christians I know. Sometimes, we put ourselves on the sidelines, but Jesus hasn't changed. If we give Him a chance, He will raise us back to new life and make us strong again. Are we going to wallow in our sins or let the Lord forgive us and move on?

Thomas allowed God to forgive him. When Thomas met with the rest of the disciples, something amazing took place—Jesus was there, and He forgave him. Thomas became a leader, an ordinary giant, who planted churches in Asia.[29] Perhaps tens of thousands came to know Christ because of him. He doubted for a while, but Jesus brought him back to new life. Jesus accepted him with all of his strengths and weaknesses.

I try not to let what others say or do affect my faith; I live for Jesus Christ. I want to maintain my passion for Him because He's the one who is perfect, who set me free and forgave all my sins—past, present, and future. It's all because of His blood.

Jesus wants a relationship with us even though we might disappoint him periodically. He knew all about me before I received Him, and He saved me anyway.

Thomas grew discouraged, but Jesus didn't get angry. Jesus doesn't rebuke honest questions. Thomas was a curious soul. It's okay to ask questions. Remember Job in the Old Testament? He was so badly hurt; he'd lost his fortune, his family, and his health (Job 1:13–22; 2:1–10). It was easy to question God. God listened to all his questions and said:

> Where were you when I laid the earth's foundation? Tell me, if you understand. Who marked off its dimensions? Surely you know! Who stretched a measuring line across it? On what were its footings set, or who laid its cornerstone—while the morning stars sang together and all the angels shouted for joy?
>
> —Job 38:4–7

It was as if God was saying, "I don't think I need any help from you. I've got this." So it is with God and Thomas, and likewise with God and us. Author and Bible teacher Steve Brown describes God's response this way:[30]

> Jesus gave an evidential answer. There is evidence for the Truth, for the veracity of the Christian faith. It is credible, it hangs together and it is open to questioning. God isn't dead. He still speaks in the evidence He has so graciously condescended to give us. When you waver, it is often because you doubt. If you doubt, it may be because you simply haven't looked down into the well of Truth.

Brown reminds us we have an evidence-based faith. God's not going anywhere. I love hearing about scientists and thinkers who have come to Christ. Once they get it, they become absolute believers due to the veracity of scientific evidence they encounter about the Bible and Jesus Christ.

Jesus could have left Thomas where he was, but He said, "No, I want you [Thomas] to believe." Jesus says something wonderful for all of us: "...blessed are those who have not seen and yet have believed" (John 20:29). He invites all of us to believe, even though we can't see Him.

Thomas grew discouraged, but Jesus still saved him. Jesus offers redemption to those who believe. What is redemption? I used to live in Louisville, Kentucky, and downtown was an area called Market Street. According to historians, this is where slaves would be put up for sale and people would bid for them. Imagine you were a free person living in that era who saw a person of color and bid for that slave. At the end of the bidding, you won the auction and the slave was yours. You said to the slave, "You are now my property." The slave might have said, "What do you want me to do?" Imagine if you replied, "I bid on you so you may go free." Can you imagine the feeling that slave would have? You invested your money, your treasure, in that slave, and then told the person that he or she was free to go anywhere.

That's exactly what Jesus did. He redeemed us. We were on the slave market of sin, and He shed His blood to purchase our salvation. He paid the price. When we received Him, He said, "Now you are free to live for me." Are we living for Christ?

Thomas had to learn how to believe again, not just to be passionate. In many ways, it's easy to be passionate about something but not believe in it. The question is, do we believe? Thomas needed to believe, not only in the concept of salvation, but in the Person of salvation—Jesus

Christ. A lot of people may believe in or be passionate about the church, a pastor, baptism, the concept of Christianity, or that our country is a Christian nation—many great things. We can talk about the Lord yet not be a believer. Do we truly believe?

God doesn't force us to believe; He allows us to believe. He calls us and knocks on our heart's door, begging us to believe.

Walking in Thomas' Footsteps

Events and circumstances caused Thomas to become discouraged in his faith and doubt. Yet, Jesus called him in the midst of his discouragement. Even though he doubted, Thomas experienced Jesus' peace and patience (John 20:26–27). When Thomas was confronted with Jesus' evidence, the only thing he could say was, "My Lord and my God" (John 20:28). Jesus accepted Thomas' confession of faith and saved him.

Thomas might not seem like much of a giant of the Christian faith. But he set an example for us by having the courage—in the midst of his doubt—to ask Jesus questions, come back to Jesus, and have a conversation with Him. When we ask God tough questions, He will give us answers, life changing answers. God wants interaction with us; He wants relationship. Our God is real, and Thomas knew that. He believed, and it changed hearts all over the world.

Jesus invites us to believe. He wants us to have fuel for our fires, evidence to believe, and strength for the journey God leads us on. Even our doubt and discouragement can become a light to guide others to Jesus. It all starts with believing in the name and work of Jesus Christ.

WORKBOOK

Chapter Seven Questions

Question: When in your life have you had great passion for Christ? Has anything happened to dampen your enthusiasm? If so, what? How has this impacted your walk with Christ? Are you ready to come to Christ for forgiveness and renewal, or have you put yourself on the sidelines out of guilt and perfectionism?

Question: Jesus wants a relationship with us even though we might disappoint Him periodically. Think of other meaningful relationships in your life. How can these actually grow stronger as you fight through times of doubt and discord? How can this be true in your relationship with Christ as well?

_____

_____

_____

_____

_____

_____

_____

_____

_____

_____

Question: What are some hard questions you have asked of God? How has He answered your doubts, frustrations, anger, fears, and pain? How has He taken you from unbelieving to believing?

_____

_____

_____

_____

_____

_____

_____

_____

_____

_____

_____

_____

Action: Who do you know who is struggling with disappointment, discouragement, or disillusionment in their Christian walk right now? Send them a note or take them to lunch. Share with them how you have seen God's faithfulness and His work in and through your own times of discouragement.

Chapter Seven Notes

CHAPTER EIGHT

John Mark—A Quitter

When Barnabas and Saul had finished their mission, they returned from Jerusalem, taking with them John, also called Mark.

Now in the church at Antioch there were prophets and teachers: Barnabas, Simeon called Niger, Lucius of Cyrene, Manaen (who had been brought up with Herod the tetrarch) and Saul. While they were worshiping the Lord and fasting, the Holy Spirit said, "Set apart for me Barnabas and Saul for the work to which I have called them." So after they had fasted and prayed, they placed their hands on them and sent them off.

The two of them, sent on their way by the Holy Spirit, went down to Seleucia and sailed from there to Cyprus. When they arrived at Salamis, they proclaimed the word of God in the Jewish synagogues. John was with them as their helper.

They traveled through the whole island until they came to Paphos. There they met a Jewish sorcerer and false prophet named Bar-Jesus, who was an attendant of the proconsul, Sergius Paulus. The proconsul, an intelligent man, sent for Barnabas and Saul because he wanted to hear the word of God. But Elymas the sorcerer (for that is what his name means) opposed them and tried to turn the proconsul from the faith. Then Saul, who was also called Paul, filled with the Holy Spirit, looked straight at Elymas and said, "You are a child of the devil and an enemy of everything that is right! You are full of all kinds of deceit and trickery. Will you never stop perverting the right ways of the Lord? Now the hand of the Lord is against you. You are going to be blind for a time, not even able to see the light of the sun."

Immediately mist and darkness came over him, and he groped about, seeking someone to lead him by the hand. When the proconsul saw what had happened, he believed, for he was amazed at the teaching about the Lord.

From Paphos, Paul and his companions sailed to Perga in Pamphylia, where John left them to return to Jerusalem.

—Acts 12:25–13:13

Growing up, Elizabeth looked forward to Sunday church services with her mother. Elizabeth enjoyed the worship songs and Sunday school stories. Soon her mother stopped going to church—Elizabeth was never quite sure if it was her mother or her father's idea—but the departure led to Elizabeth not wanting anything to do with God. She even told her friends that she'd rather not talk about God. Elizabeth never felt the need to turn to God after she married and left home.

Her mother's tragic death at sea did nothing to restore Elizabeth's trust in God, and later, after her father died, she wondered if perhaps he was the one who had pulled the family away from church. Now Elizabeth is searching for something—and she hasn't found it yet. She wonders if God would even listen if she turned to Him? Elizabeth isn't sure. When her family quit going to church, she quit on God. Could He take her back?

Throughout history, many people have turned away from God and failed in the church. John Mark was a New Testament believer who quit (Acts 15:38). He failed, but the Lord allowed him to have an amazing comeback.

Lessons from John Mark

In Acts 12:25, Barnabas and Paul left Jerusalem, taking John Mark with them. He traveled with Paul and Barnabas to Cyprus, then when Paul and his companions sailed to Pisidian Antioch, John Mark left them to return to Jerusalem (Acts 13:13). He left the mission field in the midst of Paul's missionary journey—after they encountered a sorcerer and false prophet, and before Paul preached in Pisidian Antioch. God was doing great things, but John Mark went home.

Eventually John Mark became involved in the church again preaching the gospel, and at the end of Paul's life, Paul asked for the same person who had left him: "Only Luke is with me. Get Mark and bring him with you, because he is helpful to me in my ministry" (2 Timothy 4:11). John Mark made a complete turnaround; he came back.

Through more than thirty years of pastoring, I've seen a lot of people go through highs and lows. Every church has similar examples. Some people are like sprinters— they start fast, then the first hurdle comes along, they can't quite jump it, and they quit. Some people are on fire early in their Christian lives, then become tempted, and fall. The next thing you know, they're out of church and avoiding me at the store. What have I done? Nothing. What

Satan has done is another question. The important thing to remember is John Mark returned.

John Mark was a quitter who had great training. John Mark had a solid foundation. His mother was a believer and a godly woman (Acts 12:12). Those of us who have had one or two Christian parents who raised us in the church are blessed, particularly at this time when so many families are split apart. For many people, the church is one more activity, instead of the centerpiece of their lives. John Mark's family helped host the church in Jerusalem in their home. His cousin was Barnabas (Colossians 4:10), the son of encouragement (Acts 4:36), one of the most positive people you could ever meet.

John Mark started out well, went on a missionary tour, established churches on Cyprus, and then quit. But God didn't give up on him. Barnabas didn't give up on him (Acts 15:39), and Paul didn't give up on him (2 Timothy 4:11).

I remember holding my children minutes after they were born. There's nothing more precious. That intense love I felt for them in that moment has consistently reminded me to raise them to know God. We should strive to give our families the best opportunities for spiritual success, which includes family worship experiences, establishing proper boundaries, and maintaining wholesome discipline. We are to teach our children boundaries and implement consequences when those boundaries are crossed. It's important we as parents demonstrate discipline in our families and pray for and encourage them to always come back to God.

John Mark was a quitter who failed in serving Jesus.

John Mark failed in his service to the Lord. There are many possible reasons; perhaps he didn't count the cost. Jesus said a builder first counts the cost before building (Luke 14:25–30). We needn't be embarrassed by getting started and then stopping. It's important to count the cost, and start where we can. What we do for Jesus will cost us something in our relationships and in other areas of life. When I was first called to ministry, the pastor didn't say, "We want you to preach a sermon tonight." I started with teaching middle school boys. I guess he thought if I could get through teaching young, teen boys, I could get through anything, and he was right. I enjoyed teaching them. They were full of questions, and we had a great encounter every Sunday morning. I preached in church within a couple of years, and then the pastor asked me to help start a mission. I got involved in preaching and leading and later became a pastor. From my beginnings as a youth minister, I did my best to be obedient to each opportunity.

We start wherever the Lord opens the door. Perhaps we have mentoring to help us get there. But it's important to count the cost. Maybe John Mark hadn't done this.

Some people aren't ready for service. Perhaps John Mark wasn't ready to do all the things God wanted him to do. In ministry, I see some people launch out without proper preparation. A person can't be a dentist just because he or she wants to help people with their teeth—without training all that can be done is to give people a toothbrush. It takes training to run an IT program, to be a teacher, to enter many different professions—and training is just as important in the church.

Sometimes people have impure motives and they fail. It's hard to hide in church. We need to encourage, equip, and enrich those who want to serve in the church. Paul felt John Mark hadn't done that; he had gone home (Acts 15:38). As Christians, we serve the Lord through our words and deeds. Too many of us want to leave without paying the price. Preparation is the key, and it's in those hours of preparation that God begins to mold and shape us into the people He wants us to be. Can you imagine what it was like for Paul and his companions to have John Mark leave the mission field and go home?

A seminary administrator told a story about a promising student who failed in seminary. He succumbed to temptation and violated the rules of conduct. The administrator helped the young man gather his things and drove him from the school to the airport. They probably said only two or three words the entire time. The student had failed his family, himself, the Lord, and the institution. That's a tough place to be.

Some reading this may be there right now: a past deacon no longer serving the Lord, someone who used to lead worship or sing on a worship team isn't active any longer, a Sunday school teacher or youth leader stopped serving and never returned. What happened? Most of us have our stories. Did we not count the cost? Were we not ready for the assignment God gave us?

The student and the administrator arrived at the airport. He hugged the young man and said, "You know what? God can still use you one day." The administrator didn't think about the boy for years until about fifteen years later when he received a phone call. The young man had started a church for people who had failed, like him. He had finished his schooling online and another pastor helped him. The boy had repented, God restored him, and he started a church from nothing. Today, almost two thousand people attend. Wow! God uses those who have been broken. *John Mark was a quitter who was redeemed and used by God.* How great was John Mark, really? Why is he included in this discussion of ordinary giants? Though he failed, God restored him and used him again. He even wrote the second book of the New Testament! This is one of the greatest stories of Christianity. We fail, but God is in the forgiving business. I'm so glad God didn't give up on me at my first failure, second, or one hundredth failure.

Many Christians know they're not where they're supposed to be. John Mark overcame a youthful mistake and became a powerful instrument of God. We can overcome our past failures. Mark wrote one of the Gospels, had a dynamic church ministry, and was helpful to Paul in his ministry. Paul asked to see John Mark one last time (2 Timothy 4:11) to thank him for his help in serving the Lord. John Mark experienced the heat and discipline of Paul's refusal to serve alongside him (Acts 15:39) and came back around to serve the Lord. God welcomes us with open arms, as He did John Mark, when we accept His loving discipline and return to Him with all our hearts.

God will restore us if we come back to Him (1 Peter 5:10; Jeremiah 15:19). John writes in his letter that if we confess our sins and see them as God sees them, He will cleanse us (1 John 1:9). God is in the restoration business. I've seen people who have failed miserably and then go on to do amazing work. Praise the Lord! We're in the kingdom-building business.

Scott was involved in the church when I first started my ministry at a particular church. Then he stopped attending, and our many attempts to bring him back failed. But one Sunday evening, near the end of my tenure at that church, Scott came in and sat near the back. When I gave an invitation, he almost ran down the aisle. He grabbed my shoulders, hugged me, and said, "I've sinned, I've sinned. Can God forgive me?" I didn't ask for details but told him he needed to confess his sins. We knelt down at the altar and he prayed and prayed and prayed. For many years now, Scott has been a pillar of the church.

Many of us have a friend or family member—child or grandchild—who is wayward. Perhaps by now they're twenty or thirty years old. Don't stop praying for them. Believe God can redeem them and transform them. John Mark is a great example.

When we fail, we may think, "If others knew what I've done they wouldn't want to talk to me." I've heard people say, "If I walked into your church, the roof would fall in." We're all sinners. The Bible says that "all have sinned and fall short of the glory of God" (Romans 3:23) and "the wages of sin is death, but the gift of God is eternal life in Christ Jesus our Lord" (Romans 6:23). God in His great mercy will save us (Titus 3:5), no matter what we've done, if we confess to Him.

When Jesus died on the cross, He stretched out His arms for all humanity. He had each of us on His mind. We've all sinned and felt shame or reproach. I don't know what your life has been, and I don't need to know. But I do know that God can restore anyone. Come home to Jesus Christ today.

Walking in John Mark's Footsteps

Christians are never whole unless they have a close relationship with God the Father, Jesus the Son, and the person of the Holy Spirit. The church needs each of us to use our gifts and training, all the things God has given us and uniquely equipped us to do.

Each of us has been trained and gifted to do something; we all have at least one gift. God wants us to use our training and gifts for Him in ministry. If we fall down, He wants us to get up and try again. John Mark quit while serving Jesus on the mission field. Later he returned to God, eager to serve again and give his life to ministry. His willingness to come back to God marks him as an ordinary giant.

We look up to people who are willing to learn and move forward after they make mistakes. These ordinary giants can teach us the benefits they've experienced from reinstating God as the captain of their ship. They can help us steer a straight course in our lives, so even if we've failed or quit in the past, we can turn back to God. When we do, God will restore us and use us to lead others to Him.

WORKBOOK

Chapter Eight Questions

Question: How would you describe your faith foundation? Were one or both of your parents believers? Did you attend a Bible-believing church as a child? Were you young or old when you received Christ? What pastors, authors, and fellow believers have influenced your growth in Christ over the years?

_____

_____

_____

_____

_____

_____

_____

_____

_____

_____

Question: Describe a time that you failed God, quit in a ministry or mission He gave you, or walked away from the church and/or your faith. Or, describe a time that you were tempted to do so but stayed faithful. If you relate to John Mark, what caused you to quit? If you stayed faithful, what motivated you to keep going? How can you share your experience to encourage others who want to give up?

_____

_____

_____

_____

_____

_____

_____

_____

_____

_____

_____

_____

Question: What is something that God is calling you to do in service to Him? Have you counted the cost of obedience—what is it? Have you prepared and trained for this ministry? How should you do so? What are your motives for desiring this ministry? Are they for God's glory or your own fulfillment?

_____

_____

_____

_____

_____

_____

_____

_____

_____

_____

_____

_____

Action: If you are in a place of failure, spend time in prayer this week and talk to a wise, Christian leader or mentor this week about how you can experience God's restoration in your life.

Or, if you are thriving, encourage a younger believer that there is forgiveness and another chance. Share Philippians 1:6 and the story of John Mark. Consider sharing your own story (or that of another believer you know or from church history) of how God restored you and used you after failure.

Chapter Eight Notes

CHAPTER NINE

Peter—The Courageous One

Immediately Jesus made the disciples get into the boat and go on ahead of him to the other side, while he dismissed the crowd. After he had dismissed them, he went up on a mountainside by himself to pray. Later that night, he was there alone, and the boat was already a considerable distance from land, buffeted by the waves because the wind was against it.

Shortly before dawn Jesus went out to them, walking on the lake. When the disciples saw him walking on the lake, they were terrified. "It's a ghost," they said, and cried out in fear.

But Jesus immediately said to them: "Take courage! It is I. Don't be afraid." "Lord, if it's you," Peter replied, "tell me to come to you on the water." "Come," he said.

Then Peter got down out of the boat, walked on the water and came toward Jesus. But when he saw the wind, he was afraid and, beginning to sink, cried out, "Lord, save me!" Immediately Jesus reached out his hand and caught him. "You of little faith," he said, "why did you doubt?" And when they climbed into the boat, the wind died down. 33 Then those who were in the boat worshiped him, saying, "Truly you are the Son of God."

—Matthew 14:22–33

Jason enters groups and situations with contagious enthusiasm and greets everyone he encounters with a huge grin. As he goes about his daily tasks—taking the children to school, stopping by the store, putting gas in the car—he leaps into any conversation opportunity. Jason loves to meet new people and tell them about Jesus. He is also quick to take on new projects in ministry and often finds new ways to serve. We look up to ordinary giants, like Jason, who aren't afraid to share their love for Jesus. Like Jesus' disciple Peter, they lead us by example.

Lessons from Peter

Peter was courageous in many ways. People who have courage are not only brave, they are also fearless. They act in the face of their fears. When the soldiers came for Jesus the night before His trial, Malchus came at Jesus. What did Peter do? He acted in spite of his fear, taking out his sword and chopping off the servant's ear (John 18:10). Jesus placed the ear back on and healed the servant's injury (Luke 22:51).

Earlier in Jesus' ministry, the disciples went ahead of Jesus across the lake. A storm came up and Jesus walked on the water to them. He assured them He was not a ghost, saying, "Take courage! It is I. Don't be afraid" (Matthew 14:25–27). Jesus came to the disciples in their fear to literally be their captain.

"'Lord, if it's you,' Peter replied, 'tell me to come to you on the water.'… Then Peter got down out of the boat, walked on the water and came toward Jesus." (Matthew 14:28–29). Peter had courage in the face of fear to defy the laws of physics. He's the only person, other than Jesus, in the world, in the whole history of humanity, who has ever walked on water. *Peter was courageous when he got out of the boat.* Peter had courage to get out of the boat. I love that, because so many of us are still bound by our fears. We often need a nudge to step out and do something we've always wanted to do. All of the disciples in the boat that day were afraid, but Peter had enough courage to get out of the boat. This is important, because some of us need to get out of the boat in a spiritual sense. Fear holds us back from answering God's call. Some He calls to be pastors. Some need to become missionaries. He's calling some to serve as youth pastors. We hold back because we're afraid.

John Ortberg, author and pastor of Menlo Church, said, "Getting out of the boat was Peter's great gift to Jesus; the experience of walking on water was Jesus' great gift to Peter."[31] Jesus wants all of us, not part of us. He wants us to have so much confidence in Him that we can do what seems impossible.

At one point, I served as a young-adult minister for thirty or forty young adults. We planned a white-water rafting trip down the New River in West Virginia. One young lady was afraid and said, "No way." We persuaded her to try, and she reluctantly said yes. It took two or three hours to get there, with her hesitating all the way. When we got to the staging area with the instructors in the boat, they said, "We have to tell you this. Two weeks ago, we lost someone down the New River." The river had surged after the spring season, and it was their first fatality.

The guides reassured us, and we started rafting down.

We got two hours into a six-hour adventure and nothing out of the ordinary had happened. Then they told us the most challenging part was ahead. Sure enough, our raft capsized. We all bobbed back up in our life jackets, except for one person—the girl who had expressed such fear. Somehow, she got trapped under a rock at the side. My heart sank, but a minute later she floated out, alive. I thought she would scold me afterward, but she said, "I'm so glad I went on this trip. I don't think I'll do it again, but I conquered one of my fears." What fears do we face in serving the Lord?

Peter was courageous when he kept his eyes on Jesus. For those few seconds, or minutes, when Peter walked on water, the Bible says he had his eyes fixed on Jesus. He kept looking and listening to the Lord. We must do the same. Satan is always looking for ways to make us fall. He wants us to stop halfway. He wants us to fail to complete what God has called us to do. Well-known pastor Charles Stanley said, "Opportunities are always lost when we let fear overrule our faith."[32] When we keep our eyes on Jesus, we can do amazing things. Perhaps even the impossible.

Some fear is good and healthy. When we have children, we tell them, "Don't go close to the road because there are cars." We instill fear in our children to keep them safe. That's good fear. In some ways it's good to be fearful of God. We stay mindful of God's judgment and hell, because there really is a place where people go who don't believe in Jesus Christ.

Some fear is unhealthy, but we can overcome our unhealthy fears when we keep our eyes on Jesus. God can help people overcome the fear and uncertainty they face in giving up addictions. I know people who are overwhelmed by a gambling habit; they're afraid because they owe everybody so much money.

We can place solid habits in place to help us keep our eyes on Jesus and keep our faith from sinking. Though people can hide behind any of these outward behaviors, these habits can also help us keep our lives on a straight course: going to church every week, giving tithes and offerings, giving our time or abilities, reading the Bible, praying with and for others, being a witness of what God has done in and for us. When some of our good habits begin to falter and our faith starts to sink, Jesus stretches His hand out to us; He wants us to succeed in our Christian life.

Peter was courageous when he called out to Jesus in faith. Jesus rescued Peter when he cried out for help (Matthew 14:30–31). When we stop living the best life we can for God, we're going to start sinking. It happens to any of us who don't keep our eyes on Jesus.

Peter walked on water. He got out of the boat; he tried to do something great and he did. Everything went well as long as he was watching Jesus. Isn't that how it is with us?

When we are living for God, life is great. We love coming to worship, we listen to and apply the pastor's message, we read our Bibles, pray, give, and tell others what God is doing. But then something comes along, for example, summer. Maybe we miss two weeks of church because we go on vacation and then decide not to get up in time to attend church the third week. By the fourth week—well, next thing we know, we've missed two months. We think, "*No one's called me. I guess they don't miss me there. I don't get anything out of the Bible, anyway; it's too hard to understand.*" When we keep our eyes on Jesus, we can do amazing things. But we start to sink and fail when He isn't our focus. Guess what? We need to take action.

Peter did the right thing. He said, "Lord, save me!" And Jesus reached out His hand and pulled him up (Matthew 14:30–31). The Lord has long arms and there's no place He can't reach you.

Evangelical pastor and radio preacher Charles Swindoll said, "[God] is able to take your life with all of the heartache, all of the pain, all of the regret, all of the missed opportunities, and use you for His glory."[33] He's able to do all that! That's our God. Peter took his eyes off Jesus and looked at the storm, heard the thunder, and started to sink. That's what will happen to us. But he said those words many of us refuse to say, "Lord, help me!" We need to be courageous and say those words because we need His help to keep our eyes on Him.

We typically think about using those three words only when something goes wrong. That's what happened to George recently. He was driving over the speed limit and saw blue and red flashing lights in the rearview mirror. George may have said, "Lord, help me." A good thought, but I imagine God might say, "You have to suffer the consequence if you go over seventy." If our marriage is in trouble, we can say, "Lord, help us." When the money runs out before the end of the month, we can say, "Lord, help us."

Other disciples were in the boat with Peter. They

preached, spread the gospel and later started churches and wrote some of the New Testament books. But they didn't walk on water. Before we throw too many stones at Peter for other mistakes, consider what he did in this situation. He stepped out with a miraculous faith.

Walking in Peter's Footsteps

Peter had courage to trust Jesus and step out of the boat. He was fearless. He walked on water. Sometimes, Jesus calls us out of our comfort zones to follow Him in faith. He might even call us to walk on water—to do what seems impossible! As long as he kept his eyes on Jesus, Peter maintained his courage. We can do all kinds of brave and bold things for Jesus when we constantly look to Him.

When we take our eyes off Jesus, we miss out on blessings. He wants us to say, "Help me, Lord," and He'll help us follow Him in faith to where He wants us to be. Last night I went to a community dinner for the homeless—a little out of my comfort zone. I was glad to see so many people serving others in need. I would have missed out on a real blessing if I hadn't gone down there.

But here's what I love about Peter. He had courage to call on Jesus even after he took his eyes off Him. Like other ordinary giants we've observed, Peter humbled himself to turn back to Christ in faith even after he made a mistake. His error in judgment—taking his eyes off Jesus—caused him to sink. The same thing happens to us, and we can miss out on God's blessings when we take our eyes off Him.

In this case, Peter let himself down when he took his

eyes off Jesus. At other times in his relationship with Jesus, he let the Lord down. When we get things wrong and let God down, He will bring us back if we ask Him. Jesus restored Peter and brought him back more than once, and Peter learned the lesson. Peter became a bold preacher and leader of the church after Jesus' ascension. He became a champion of and for Jesus. We need more people like Peter today.

WORKBOOK

Chapter Nine Questions

Question: Imagine you were with the disciples on the day that Jesus walked on water. Would you have asked Jesus to let you walk on water, or would you have stayed safely in the boat? If you would have stayed in the boat, what fears might have held you back? Are these healthy or unhealthy fears? How do these same fears keep you from being courageous for Christ today?

_____

_____

_____

_____

_____

_____

_____

Question: What is something that you have been able to courageously do by keeping your eyes on Jesus? When is a time that you have called out to Jesus to rescue you from a situation where you were sinking because you took your eyes off of Him?

_____

_____

_____

_____

_____

_____

_____

_____

_____

_____

Question: What does it take to keep your eyes on Jesus? What are some practical ways that you can keep your focus on Him instead of on a dire circumstance or distracting situation around you?

_____

_____

_____

_____

_____

_____

_____

_____

_____

_____

_____

_____

_____

Action: Choose a ministry opportunity through your church that is outside your experience or comfort zone. Perhaps a mission trip, a leadership role, or a ministry to a different age group or ethnic group than you have worked with before. Ask God to prepare your heart, keep your focus on Him, and give you courage as you navigate this opportunity.

Chapter Nine Notes

CHAPTER TEN

Philip—The Inviter

The next day Jesus decided to leave for Galilee. Finding Philip, he said to him, "Follow me."

Philip, like Andrew and Peter, was from the town of Bethsaida. Philip found Nathanael and told him, "We have found the one Moses wrote about in the Law, and about whom the prophets also wrote—Jesus of Nazareth, the son of Joseph."

"Nazareth! Can anything good come from there?" Nathanael asked.

"Come and see," said Philip.

When Jesus saw Nathanael approaching, he said of him, "Here truly is an Israelite in whom there is no deceit."
—John 1:43–47

Ordinary giants invite and lead other people to Jesus Christ. When we invite, we ask someone to do something or go somewhere. In this case, we want to follow Philip's example to invite someone to meet Jesus, to join us in our walk with God. But when it comes to reaching un-churched people, we have a lot of excuses for why we aren't doing it. Thom Rainer, founder and CEO of Church Answers, said there are six excuses Christians give for not reaching out to unbelievers:[34]

1. That's what we pay our pastor to do.

2. People in our church are not evangelistic.

3. Our denomination does not help us.

4. We emphasize evangelism once a year in our church.

5. I don't know anyone who is not a Christian.

6. We don't have the resources.

But any bits of truth in our excuses do not let us off the hook. For example, the fifth reason is true for many of us. But if I go to Walmart and wear my shirt with the church logo, I could have one hundred conversations if I stayed there an hour or two and took the initiative to talk with people.

Lessons from Philip

The apostle John introduces us to Philip, one of Jesus' disciples. "The next day Jesus decided to leave for Gali-lee. Finding Philip, he said to him, 'Follow me'" (John 1:43). Philip had heard about Jesus and was ready to become a disciple. And he was excited enough about it to find a friend and say, "Come and see" (John 1:46).

We meet people and get to know them, and they become our friends. If after a time, we don't talk to them about God, how close are we to God? And how much do we care about our friends? *Philip invited because he knew and demonstrated the importance of salvation.* Philip invited his friend to come to Jesus. He gave an evangelistic witness; he practiced evangelism. I want to define evangelism because Christians often use big, church words, and others may not know what they mean. There's a difference between witnessing and evangelizing. One critical aspect of evangelism is to present the gospel of Jesus Christ through our words and actions *and* ask for a response: "Do you want Jesus to come into your life?" When we ask that question, it makes our witness evangelistic. We witness when we tell others what God has done for us and that Jesus Christ is our Savior. God wants all people to come to Him (2 Peter 3:9), and we help build the kingdom when our witness is evangelistic.

Philip gave a great evangelistic witness. He said, "Come and see." As Christians, it should be natural to invite our friends to meet Jesus. The cure for death is salvation in Jesus Christ. Every one of us is going to die at some point, unless the Lord comes back, but anyone who believes in Jesus has everlasting life. When we die, we will be taken to heaven and come into the very presence of God (Philippians 1:22–24; 2 Corinthians 5:8).

I've been with families hundreds of times as they face illness or even death. Hospice nurses share that it's a peaceful transition when a believer dies. That peace, the assurance of salvation, is lacking when an unbeliever dies.

Unfortunately, I've witnessed this, too.

We have the opportunity to share the greatest news on earth. Sometimes, we need to be confronted with this reminder. Whom have you led to Jesus in the past year? Has your witness been evangelistic? Have you told others what Jesus has done for you and asked them for a response—to come and meet Jesus for themselves? We can't do the work of the Holy Spirit. Though we ask, they're not going to come just because we ask; the Holy Spirit draws them. But we have to do our part by asking.

Many churches across our country appear to have it all—programs for every segment of society, mission outreaches, beautiful sanctuaries, fun events—but they lack the fire to bring people in to meet Jesus. We each can change this

Churches consist of imperfect people, and people disappoint and hurt each other. Sometimes, these hurts cause churches to split or even cease to exist. But if we focus on Jesus and invite others to come and see what He has done, this strengthens our churches.

Philip found Nathanael and brought him to Jesus. It was natural for him to tell somebody. Philip experienced life with Jesus and His death and resurrection (Acts 1:13), and he understood the importance of salvation through Christ. We have a cure for death because of Jesus.

Philip invited because he cared about people. We know Philip reached out to Nathanael. Philip's name means "friend," but that doesn't mean he had perfected the role of caring for and inviting others.[35] He was an imperfect person; like us, he had some growing to do. By the middle of Jesus' ministry, crowds were following Him.

John sets the stage for one of Jesus' miracles: "Jesus went up on a mountainside and sat down with his disciples. ... When Jesus looked up and saw a great crowd coming toward him, he said to Philip, 'Where shall we buy bread for these people to eat?'" (John 6:3, 5)

It was natural for Jesus to ask Philip this question, because Philip was from the nearby community of Bethsaida and would know the best way to feed the crowds (John 1:44).[36] He may have known many people in the crowd and cared enough about them to invite them to hear Jesus. Jesus set an example for the disciples, especially Philip, because He was concerned about the people's welfare.[37]

As we look at glimpses of Philip in the Gospel of John, we see one aspect of his personality was to seek truth by investigating facts. Jesus had compassion on the people and modeled this as He posed the question, which was "only to test" Philip (John 6:6). He wanted Philip to consider whether he truly had compassion on the people. Philip answered Jesus' question with numbers: *if* they could find enough food to feed them all, it would cost too much money for everyone to have even a little!

In this short question and answer session, Jesus wanted to teach Philip the power He held over nature, over everything. Philip was so engaged with his answer to the question, with the numbers, he forgot about the people themselves. This happens today, too. Sometimes, we get so concerned about others' needs that we forget to invite them to meet Jesus. That's a danger in missions: caring for the need but not completing the mission and being evangelistic by telling them about Jesus.

Erwin Lutzer, a former pastor of Moody Church, said,

"Mass communication can aid in personal evangelism and the development of Christians, but it cannot be a substitute for the world seeing the truth lived *through us*."[38] In addition to telling people about the love of God, we also need to show them through our actions.

Author Matt Chandler said it this way: "...relational evangelism? Go for it, as long as it turns into actual evangelism. You hanging out having a beer with your buddy so he can see that Christians are cool is not what we're called to do."[39]

Jesus' teaching in John 6 ends with a visible object lesson: He is more than enough to meet the physical need. In His teaching the next day, He extends the lesson to include His all-sufficiency for spiritual needs.

Philip grasped part of this truth; he found Nathanael and invited him to meet Jesus.

Philip invited Jesus to teach him more about the kingdom. The next time we encounter Philip, he has participated in the Passover meal with Jesus and the other disciples in the upper room (John 13). It a momentous evening for the disciples, as Jesus serves them and also predicts betrayal and denial. Jesus offers them comfort and more than one promise and invites them to follow Him into the presence of God the Father (John 14:6).

If Philip is going to continue to invite people to meet Jesus, he wants to make sure he's got his facts straight. He questions the Lord about the kingdom, asking Jesus to teach him more: "Lord, show us the Father and that will be enough for us" (John 14:8). In other words, "Help us to see God, your heavenly Father, and that will be sufficient for us to help others come to know God as well."[40]

Even today we struggle to wrap our minds around this conversation between Jesus and His disciples; Philip sought answers to difficult questions. "Jesus answered: 'Don't you know me, Philip, even after I have been among you such a long time? Anyone who has seen me has seen the Father. How can you say, "Show us the Father?"'" (John 14:9). Are you scratching your head in puzzlement right about now? I am.

It's okay to question God. We see Jesus patiently talking with the disciples, listening to their questions. When we talk with unbelievers, these kinds of questions are bound to come up. There are two questions I often hear when I talk with non-believers:

1. *Why is there suffering?* I don't have the answer. I know I'm a Christian, and I've had cancer and cardiac issues. There are non-Christians who have cancer and cardiac issues. It rains on the just and the unjust alike (Matthew 5:45).

2. *Why is Christianity exclusive?* Jesus says, "I am the way and the truth and the life. No one comes to the Father except through me" (John 14:6). Why? The Bible explains Jesus was the Messiah, the Promised One. Here's how we know Jesus is the only One in the world who has ever been—or ever will be—the Messiah: prophecy. We see the story of Jesus foretold throughout the Old Testament, and the Book of Revelation tells us what Jesus will do in the days to come.

Our willingness to discuss these and other hard questions with honesty, with Bible in hand, can help open the door for us to invite others to know Jesus.

Walking in Philip's Footsteps

Philip is an ordinary giant who met Jesus and, through the Holy Spirit, understood Jesus was the one his heart and soul sought. Philip went to Nathanael and said, "We have found the one" (John 1:45)! He knew enough about Jesus to know what he had found was too good not to share. It was important to him to seek out and find Nathanael to tell him this good news. Is Jesus so important to us that we go looking for people to invite? "Come and see," I want you to meet Jesus.

Philip invited Jesus to teach him; he had an open heart and mind—and a lot to learn! After he invited a few people from his hometown to hear Jesus speak, he learned there's a lot more to inviting and caring about people. It's important to not lose sight of the people in the process of figuring out how to meet their needs.

More than their physical needs, people have spiritual needs of eternal consequence. Philip must have grasped at least a glimmer of that concept when he asked Jesus to show the disciples the Father. He understood Jesus was the one who could show them the way to God, even if he didn't understand the relationship between Jesus and the Father. He was willing to consider Jesus as the captain of his ship and learn from Him. Do we invite Jesus and the Holy Spirit to teach us more about the kingdom? Will we stand firm on the foundation of our relationship with Jesus to invite others to meet and get to know Him?

Philip shows us what it means to follow Jesus. He had a desire to bring his friend Nathanael to meet Jesus. Those who invite others to come to Jesus are ordinary giants in God's kingdom, as they fulfill the commission Jesus gave His disciples in Matthew 28:19–20. Perhaps there's something wrong if we never have a desire to lead someone to Jesus or to talk to others about the Lord. Is He the closest thing to your heart or the furthest thing from your mind? Ordinary giants, people like Philip, invite people to meet their friend and Savior, Jesus Christ.

WORKBOOK

Chapter Ten Questions

Question: Looking at the list of six excuses for why Christians don't reach out to unbelievers, which one do you most often find yourself saying or thinking? What about this thinking is an excuse rather than the truth?

_____

_____

_____

_____

_____

_____

_____

_____

_____

_____

Question: How often do you intentionally witness? How often is your witness evangelistic? How do you do it and with whom do you share? Who is one person or what is one group of people whom God has put on your heart to reach for Him? How will you build a relationship with them?

_____

_____

_____

_____

_____

_____

_____

_____

_____

_____

_____

_____

Question: How can tangible care and genuine compassion help prepare people to be receptive to the gospel? What happens when believers do good works to help others but never actually share the good news? What happens when believers share the good news but never do good works to help meet needs?

_____

_____

_____

_____

_____

_____

_____

_____

_____

_____

_____

Action: Make a list of some common, hard questions that unbelievers have. Begin a study of apologetics that will help you to have an honest, humble reply for these difficult questions (a reply may not be an *answer*; there are many things that cannot be fully understood or answered on this side of eternity).

Action: Read a book or take a course on personal evangelism to make sure that you are confident and prepared to share the gospel. I personally recommend *The Case for Christ* by Lee Strobel and *Evidence That Demands a Verdict* by John McDowell and Sean McDowell, Ph.D.

Chapter Ten Notes

CHAPTER ELEVEN

Timothy—The Young Christian

In the presence of God and of Christ Jesus, who will judge the living and the dead, and in view of his appearing and his kingdom, I give you this charge: Preach the word; be prepared in season and out of season; correct, rebuke and encourage—with great patience and careful instruction. For the time will come when people will not put up with sound doctrine. Instead, to suit their own desires, they will gather around them a great number of teachers to say what their itching ears want to hear. They will turn their ears away from the truth and turn aside to myths. But you, keep your head in all situations, endure hardship, do the work of an evangelist, discharge all the duties of your ministry.

For I am already being poured out like a drink offering, and the time for my departure is near. I have fought the good fight, I have finished the race, I have kept the faith. Now there is in store for me the crown of righteousness, which the Lord, the righteous Judge, will award to me on that day—and not only to me, but also to all who have longed for his appearing.

—2 Timothy 4:1–8

A high-school football athlete from Georgia was one of the top recruits across the country. He played running back and could run like lightning. All the big football programs recruited him: Alabama, Georgia, Florida. One day he woke up with a twinge in his knee, but ignored it for a few days before telling his coach. The trainer checked it out and sent him to the doctor. He had an MRI and a team of doctors came in and said, "Son, we've got terrible news. You have a rare form of cancer and unless we take your leg, it's going to run through your whole body."

Can you imagine getting such news? He was a young man with the whole world in front of him. The chaplain came in to pray with him—he wasn't a Christian and was angry at God, at everything. He had a couple of days to decide whether or not to go ahead with the operation. He prayed some more with the chaplain who asked, "Do you want to be a Christian? I know you're angry with God, but God will walk with you and you can have a great life." The boy asked the Lord to come into his heart.

He had the operation and the doctors found a cyst instead of cancer. They told him, "The cancer wasn't cancer. Something happened over the last three or four days, and we found only a benign cyst. We didn't have to remove your leg." From his hospital bed the boy threw his hands in the air and said, "My God did this."

Lessons from Timothy

Timothy was an ordinary giant in the New Testament who was converted at a young age. He came from a mixed family: one parent was a Jew, the other a Gentile (Acts

16:1–2), yet he received Christ and became a tremendous help to the ministry. Timothy helped Paul on his second missionary journey (Philippians 2:22); he was a spiritual person and a talented speaker, a communicator of God's love (1 Thessalonians 3:2, 6). Even at a young age, Timothy learned to let God lead him (1 Timothy 4:12).

People are more likely to become Christians before the age of eighteen, so churches make a particular effort to stay engaged with young people. Timothy was young when he realized his need for salvation. The gospel message is still true today; anyone can receive the same salvation Timothy received, regardless of age. Salvation comes from Jesus Christ, not technology or video games or anything else except the love He demonstrated when He died for us on the cross.

Timothy yearned for Jesus. Young people are naturally drawn to Jesus. Why wouldn't a young person come to Him? It's unnatural if a child doesn't! As parents, we will have to give an account of how we raised our children. Did we take them to church? Did we introduce them to the Lord? How about our grandchildren? The most important seed we can sow as parents is to instill the Word of God into our children.

It's a thrill for me when little children come up and say, "Hi, Pastor French." It's awesome to know people in my church are investing in eternity by bringing their children to Jesus Christ. He's the Maker of heaven and earth; the Way, the Truth, and the Life (Psalm 115:5; John 14:6).

Jesus loves children—He loves the whole world! Kids see this more than adults; they don't have prejudice. They don't see each other's differences; they just see another person. That's exactly how it will be in heaven! There will be no distinction.

J. D. Greear said, "There is only one posture appropriate to Christ: surrendered to His Lordship, and believing that He did what He said He did. From the very beginning of their lives, I want my kids to assume that posture!"[41] He made sure his children were introduced to Jesus Christ and saved by God's grace. I can't save a soul; we can't save our children or grandchildren. Only Jesus Christ saves; our job is to introduce them to the Lord.

When Paul arrived at Timothy's hometown of Lystra, Timothy was already a disciple (Acts 16:1). Timothy was so drawn to Jesus that Paul thought he would be a help on his missionary journey (Acts 16:3). We can only wonder how young Timothy was at this point, as Paul writes to him at least ten years later saying, "Don't let anyone look down on you because you are young" (1 Timothy 4:12).

Timothy resisted temptation. Paul encouraged Timothy by saying:

> *Those who want to get rich fall into temptation and a trap and into many foolish and harmful desires that plunge people into ruin and destruction. For the love of money is a root of all kinds of evil. Some people, eager for money, have wandered from the faith and pierced themselves with many griefs. But you, man of God, flee from all this, and pursue righteousness, godliness, faith, love, endurance and gentleness.*
> —*1 Timothy 6:9-11*

Paul also advised Timothy: "Watch your life and doctrine closely. Persevere in them, because if you do, you will save both yourself and your hearers" (1 Timothy 4:16). How do we know Timothy followed Paul's advice?

> *"[Paul] sent Timothy, who is our brother and co-worker in God's service in spreading the gospel of Christ, to strengthen and encourage you in your faith, so that no one would be unsettled by these trials. ... [W]hen I could stand it no longer, I sent to find out about your faith. I was afraid that in some way the tempter had tempted you and that our labors might have been in vain. But Timothy has just now come to us from you and has brought good news about your faith and love.*
> *—1 Thessalonians 3:2-3, 5-6a*

When the believers in Macedonia faced trials and temptations, Paul left Silas and Timothy there to minister to them, so Timothy and Silas must have been strong enough in their own faith and Christian walks to help others.

We will always face temptations; it's part of the human condition. Temptation is tough, but the Bible offers hope: "God is faithful; he will not let you be tempted beyond what you can bear. But when you are tempted, he will also provide a way out so that you can endure it" (1 Corinthians 10:13).

Christians are filled with the Holy Spirit. The greatest thing the Holy Spirit does for us is to guide us, convict us, and tell us which way to go (John 16:7–15). The moment we believed we were baptized by the Holy Spirit, He came to live inside us. We have the Holy Spirit; don't let anyone tell you otherwise. With God's Spirit inside us, we know when we stray from His guidance and sin.

Those who are young in their faith, as were some of the believers in Macedonia, need ordinary giants to lead them and strengthen them as they face temptations. Those who are young in life, like Timothy was, need the encouragement of ordinary giants like Paul and others we've studied in this book. In his letters to Timothy, Paul gives valuable instruction about how to live the Christian life.

In both of his letters, as well as other places in the New Testament, Paul calls Timothy his *dear son* in the faith (2 Timothy 1:2). We can believe Paul prayed for Timothy and his ministry. In the same way, we need to stop giving prayer lip service and start praying more for our natural and spiritual children. I attended the first See You at the Pole event at our local school, a day set aside across our country for students to gather at the flagpoles of their schools before class to pray for their schools, friends, families, churches, and communities. A group of parents, students, and I circled the flagpole and held hands. Today, parents aren't always allowed to come to the See You at the Pole events, but we can still meet together informally to pray for our young people.

Timothy served God and others. Like many young people, Timothy was an enthusiastic follower of Jesus. The root meaning of the word *enthusiasm* is "possessed by a god, inspired."[42] John Wooden, the basketball coach from UCLA, believes enthusiasm to be an unequivocal cornerstone of success.[43] Enthusiasm is a largely underused technique in coaching, and it's also one of the most undervalued commodities in the church. When people first become saved, they are on fire for Jesus Christ. Young believers, regardless of age, want to tell somebody about their new faith.

I'm convinced many Christians have a lack of enthusiasm about God, Jesus, and the church. To me, the most important day of the week is Sunday, the Lord's day. But I think it's important to share the good news about Jesus Christ other times during the week as well.

Why aren't we more enthusiastic about the One we will spend the rest of our lives with, even after we die? Why aren't we more enthusiastic about the Bible? It took forty authors writing in three different languages over fifteen hundred years to compile the sixty-six books we know as the Bible. But it all has one theme: there is one true God and He promised to bring forth His Son, the Messiah. The Bible tells us He was born in Bethlehem and given the name "Jesus, because he will save his people from their sins" (Matthew 1:21). He was put in a borrowed tomb after His death on a cross, but that tomb could not hold Him (Luke 23:55). On the third day He rose again (Luke 24:1–8). Forty days later He ascended back to God the Father (Acts 1:1–3; Luke 24:51), and one day He is coming back (Hebrews 9:28). That is our God!

Why don't we want to know Him better and tell others about Him? Timothy served God and others and was an asset to Paul's ministry. He "proved himself, because as a son with his father he has served with me in the work of the gospel" (Philippians 2:22). He showed genuine concern for the believers' welfare, looking out for the interests of Jesus Christ (Philippians 2:20–21), which are to draw all men to Him for salvation (John 12:32).

We need a revolution of people of all ages who aren't afraid of giving a witness for Jesus Christ. People from all walks of life can step up and serve God and others by lead-ing youth, teaching, sharing the gospel with neighbors, or strengthening and encouraging others in their faith, as Timothy did. God wants followers who are enthusiastic for Him. He wants young people to step up and say, "We're going to serve God and others because we love Jesus."

Walking in Timothy's Footsteps

Timothy was young, but his youth worked in his favor. He was an ordinary giant. The word *giant* brings to mind someone who is larger than life. Like many young people, Timothy may have had moments when he believed he could conquer the world. Often, young people are influ-enced by their peers' enthusiasm and energy. They have confidence in the success of their endeavors and believe they can make a strong impression on people. New believ-ers—those who are young in their faith—often have similar traits: they yearn for more of Jesus and serve God and others enthusiastically. They learn to withstand trials and resist temptation with the help of strong mentors, or-dinary giants who have characteristics similar to Paul and Barnabas.

Paul encouraged Timothy, "Preach the word; be pre-pared in season and out of season; correct, rebuke and encourage—with great patience and careful instruction. … [K]eep your head in all situations, endure hardship, do the work of an evangelist" (2 Timothy 4:2, 5). Always preach the truth, and don't give in to the world. Don't give in! Don't give up! Don't give out! The Lord wants us to yearn for Him with our whole heart and to serve God and others with enthusiasm.

Regardless of our physical age, we can learn from Timothy. God gives each of His followers a part to play! A review of the principles we observe in Timothy's life will help us embrace our roles as evangelistic witnesses for Jesus, with all the fervor and enthusiasm of a new believer. Young people run toward that which they find exciting. Let's run toward Jesus with a yearning to know Him. He wants to be the *only* captain of our ship.

As Timothy served and worked in the ministry alongside Paul, we can also align ourselves with godly mentors who will help us learn to resist temptation. As we interact with other believers, we can strengthen and encourage one another in the faith to serve God and others wholeheartedly. Like young Timothy, "we are no longer to be children ... but we are to grow up in all *aspects* into Him who is the head, *even* Christ" (Ephesians 4:14a–15b NASB).

WORKBOOK

Chapter Eleven Questions

Question: What are some ways that parents, grandparents, and children's and youth workers can introduce the young people in their lives to the Lord? What are some effective means of discipleship?

_____

_____

_____

_____

_____

_____

_____

_____

_____

_____

Question: What are some temptations that Christian young people need to be more adequately prepared to face? How can those who are older in the faith help to strengthen the younger generation for these temptations and teach them to listen to the Holy Spirit? Name someone in your life who has helped you grow in your faith. How has this person influenced your walk with Jesus?

_____

_____

_____

_____

_____

_____

_____

_____

_____

_____

_____

Question: Are you helping to foster enthusiasm about serving Christ, or have you become a naysayer? Are you open to new ideas from younger believers who are "on fire" for Christ? If you are a younger believer, how are you modeling passionate love and service for the Lord?

_____

_____

_____

_____

_____

_____

_____

_____

_____

_____

_____

_____

Action: Plan a way that you will encourage a "Timothy" in your life this week and that you will show appreciation to a "Paul" who has been a mentor to you.

Chapter Eleven Notes

_____

_____

_____

_____

_____

_____

_____

_____

_____

_____

_____

_____

_____

_____

_____

_____

_____

_____

_____

_____

_____

_____

CHAPTER TWELVE

Stephen—The Risk Taker

In those days when the number of disciples was increasing, the Hellenistic Jews among them complained against the Hebraic Jews because their widows were being overlooked in the daily distribution of food. So the Twelve gathered all the disciples together and said, "It would not be right for us to neglect the ministry of the word of God in order to wait on tables. Brothers and sisters, choose seven men from among you who are known to be full of the Spirit and wisdom. We will turn this responsibility over to them and will give our attention to prayer and the ministry of the word."

This proposal pleased the whole group. They chose Stephen, a man full of faith and of the Holy Spirit; also Philip, Procorus, Nicanor, Timon, Parmenas, and Nicolas from Antioch, a convert to Judaism. They presented these men to the apostles, who prayed and laid their hands on them.

So the word of God spread. The number of disciples in Jerusalem increased rapidly, and a large number of priests became obedient to the faith.

Now Stephen, a man full of God's grace and power, performed great wonders and signs among the people. Opposition arose, however, from members of the Synagogue of the Freedmen (as it was called)—Jews of Cyrene and Alexandria as well as the provinces of Cilicia and Asia—who began to argue with Stephen. But they could not stand up against the wisdom the Spirit gave him as he spoke.

Then they secretly persuaded some men to say, "We have heard Stephen speak blasphemous words against Moses and against God."

So they stirred up the people and the elders and the teachers of the law. They seized Stephen and brought him before the Sanhedrin. They produced false witnesses, who testified, "This fellow never stops speaking against this holy place and against the law. For we have heard him say that this Jesus of Nazareth will destroy this place and change the customs Moses handed down to us."

All who were sitting in the Sanhedrin looked intently at Stephen, and they saw that his face was like the face of an angel.

—Acts 6:1–15

Ordinary giants are people who have been changed by the gospel of Jesus Christ. They aren't people with superpowers or extraordinary strength; they're ordinary people who live in a fallen, broken world but they stand tall once they encounter the supernatural love of Christ.

Nicky Cruz is an example.[44] Growing up with parents who abused him and worshiped Satan, Nicky's childhood wasn't the stuff of happy-ever-after fairy tales. As a gang member on the streets of New York, Nicky met Pastor David Wilkerson, who risked his life to tell Nicky about Jesus. David Wilkerson exemplified the same principles we see in Stephen's life: he risked everything to love Nicky Cruz, to preach the good news about Jesus, and if necessary, to die there on the streets of New York. Wilkerson said it this way, "You could cut me up into 1,000 pieces and lay them in the street. Every piece will still love you."

Nicky took the pastor's message to heart and attended one of Wilkerson's rallies where he gave his heart and life to Jesus. The teen risked everything he had ever known to declare his love for Jesus. He risked his life and left the gang scene. He risked everything to preach the love of Christ to his family, resulting in their salvation. As far as Nicky is concerned, the love he received from Jesus was worth the risk. Today, Nicky is an evangelist and head of an evangelistic Christian ministry.

Lessons from Stephen

The early church grew, and the people in need and widows were being fed by the church. This task overwhelmed the apostles, with the other work of the ministry they also did, so they decided to select deacons to oversee the food distribution. One of those selected was Stephen, "a man full of faith and of the Holy Spirit" (Acts 6:5).

Jesus touched Stephen's life, and he was "a man full of God's grace and power" (Acts 6:8), who boldly served the Lord. Sometimes, we get caught up in the routines of church life and forget about the overarching reason we go to church—Jesus Christ is alive! When we consider what Jesus has done for us, it's worth risking everything for Him.

Stephen risked everything to love people. The first thing Stephen risked was his reputation. He was willing to figuratively wait tables (Acts 6:2). Whatever Jesus asked him to do, he would do. By serving widows and those who needed food, Stephen, and the others chosen to serve, risked their standing among the believers. They served without discrimination between Jewish and non-Jewish women (Acts 6:1). We can't discriminate when we love others in the name of Jesus. We can't say, "I want only my friends to get saved. I don't want the people over there to come to my church." I want everyone to feel welcome at our church; I don't want anyone to feel this isn't a church for them. Rich or poor, black or white—they're all welcome!

Stephen treated people fairly. We can guess from his willingness to serve, he was also kindhearted. As a child, I looked up to the deacons in the church, those who served in various ways. They were kind to me, and I always remembered that. Our actions are important. Stephen's actions pointed people to the Lord; he witnessed what God had done in his life by serving others. He risked what other people might think of him and declared his faith by what he did.

One way we can risk everything to love people is to serve within our local church as Stephen did. The church asked him to participate "in the daily serving *of food* ... to serve tables" (Acts 6:1–2 NASB). Some people may think they don't need to be part of the local church to tell others about God. It's true that Christ went into the community, but Paul reminds us we "are Christ's body, and individually members of it" (1 Corinthians 12:27 NASB), in which "the whole body, being fitted and held together by what every joint supplies, according to the proper working of each individual part, causes the growth of the body for the building up of itself in love" (Ephesians 4:16 NASB).

If it wasn't for the church of Jesus Christ, this whole world would be going to hell. We are the mouthpiece of Christ, the hope that shines from doors, windows, and steeples. Our communities are better because of churches that preach the gospel.

We need to remember the church needs us. Don't wait for someone to ask. Every week there are jobs to do in the church—step up and be involved. Every Thursday afternoon, Nancy, Samuel, and Jessica come into the sanctuary and make sure everything is in place and there is no trash in the pews. Robert mows the lawn each week—it doesn't just happen. The church is the hub of the Christian's life. Everything we do for Jesus matters.

Why are some Christians not part of a local church? Part of loving people is helping them feel welcome, so they know they're right where God wants them to be. What are believers supposed to do when they move to a new community? Find a local church and be part of it. It's up to us to welcome people. Not everyone chooses to join formally, but God wants us to be actively involved in the local church (Hebrews 10:24–25).

Stephen risked everything to preach boldly. Stephen also witnessed with his words. The Bible doesn't tell us how much time passes between Stephen's early service and later boldly proclaiming the gospel. But we know he did both of these things, as later in Acts 6, we read that some men "began to argue with Stephen. But they could not stand up against the wisdom the Spirit gave him as he spoke" (Acts 6:9–10). The people "seized Stephen and brought him before the Sanhedrin" (Acts 6:12). Stephen proceeded to summarize the history of God's dealing with the Israelites (Acts 7:1–53). At the end of his speech, he proclaimed God the Father, Son, and Holy Spirit (Acts 7:54–56).

I often hear people say, "I'll do anything but don't ask me to pray aloud or give a testimony or do anything in the church that involves talking about God in front of other people, because I'd mess up." Let's face it, we all mess up at some point. God doesn't call perfect people; He calls ordinary giants. Why do we say *no* to God? Have you ever asked Him if it's okay to not talk about Him? He wants us to be witnesses with our actions and our words. What if none of us ever talked about the Lord?

How many of us are afraid to witness? It's okay to say we don't have all the answers. People respect us when we say that—they tune us out when we act like we know everything. God wants us to tell them what we do know.

We may think we can witness only through our actions, like Stephen did. But sometimes we do need to use words. All of us should be ready to give the *airplane testimony*. Within one minute, we should be able to tell a seatmate about Jesus: what our life was like before, how we met Jesus, and what our life has been like since. Spend twenty seconds on each point. It's easy! Anyone can do it with a little practice! Stephen witnessed boldly with words. If Jesus is our Lord, we need to tell others about Him. Don't be silent.

Stephen risked everything to die for Jesus. Stephen lived faithfully for Jesus, even to death. He was a martyr for his faith. What qualities did he possess that led him to risk everything for Jesus, even his life?

Stephen was full of the Holy Spirit (Acts 7:55). When we put our faith and trust in Jesus and what He did, we are baptized by the Holy Spirit and He lives inside us. We have all the Holy Spirit we need the moment we become a Christian. The question always is, does the Holy Spirit have more of us?

Stephen was full of wisdom (Acts 6:3). Former Bible teacher and writer Warren Wiersbe said, "Someone has said that knowledge is the ability to take things apart, while wisdom is the ability to put them together."[45] Stephen allowed the Holy Spirit to orchestrate his words as he talked with others.

He was full of faith (Acts 6:5), able to take on the challenges set before him. In this case, it was serving people of different backgrounds who were complaining because they were overlooked. His faith enabled him to work peacefully in a stressful situation. Stephen was full of grace (Acts 6:8). He remembered Jesus saved him. When we are full of grace, we interact with others without looking down on them.

Our understanding of God's grace enables us, like Stephen, to experience God's power (Acts 6:8). God gives us the character qualities and grace we need to do what He asks us to do. Stephen was a servant; he served as a layman, not a pastor.

Stephen's story doesn't begin with what a great man he was. It begins with him being called into a ministry of service because he was full of the Spirit and wisdom. He was an ordinary giant who risked everything because of the Spirit's work in his life. Anything Jesus asked him to do, he did, even though it led to being stoned to death. At the end, Stephen, full of the Spirit and God's grace, prayed, "Lord Jesus, receive my spirit" (Acts 7:59). Then Stephen, full of wisdom and God's grace, cried out, "Lord, do not hold this sin against them" (Acts 7:60). How many of us would risk everything, even unto death, and then forgive our persecutors?

Walking in Stephen's Footsteps

Stephen, an ordinary giant, took bold risks for Jesus Christ. His actions reflected his faith, as he risked everything to love people and serve the church. He declared his faith with his actions for the least of the local church. His words reflected his faith, as he risked his life to preach the gospel. Stephen, full of wisdom, God's grace, and power, stood up to charges from his accusers. Finally, his life and death reflected God's Spirit and grace at work in him, as he risked everything to die for Jesus.

John Newton, a former slave-trading sailor who experienced God's grace and salvation, said that "the Lord sent from on high and delivered me out of deep waters."[46] He gave his life to Jesus and asked Him to be the captain of his life.

With his life transformed by God, Newton risked his reputation as captain to love the sailors under his command by being a Christian example to them. Later he left the security of steady employment to become a minister of the gospel. Newton risked ridicule and rejection when he left his small country church to minister to the poor, the merchants, and the wealthiest and most influential people in London society. He boldly preached God's grace and Christ as Savior. He did not risk his life, but he gave his life to the gospel, and his legacy lives on in the hymns he wrote.

Who do we know who puts his or her heart, soul, and life at risk for Jesus? Ordinary giants set it all aside to follow Jesus and love and serve others. They take risks for their faith, to boldly proclaim Jesus Christ as the Son of God.

WORKBOOK

Chapter Twelve Questions

Question: What are some unglamorous jobs at church that you have done or can do? Why are these jobs important, and what are some of the hidden blessings in being a part of them?

_____

_____

_____

_____

_____

_____

_____

_____

_____

_____

Question: Are you more comfortable *doing* things in church or *talking* about the Lord? How can you become more balanced by taking a risk and stepping outside your comfort zone to serve the Lord through both your actions and your words? Who is someone that you can speak to this week about the difference Christ has made in your life?

_____

_____

_____

_____

_____

_____

_____

_____

_____

_____

Question: What are some risks that God is calling you to take? These may be risks in your reputation, career, church service, or relationships. What will you risk, in faith, for the Lord? Spend time in prayer and commitment to following Jesus, no matter the cost.

Action: Be inspired through learning about modern day martyrs. Organizations like The Voice of the Martyrs offer true stories and prayer prompts regarding the persecuted church around the world. In addition, the International Mission Board of the Southern Baptist Convention highlights missionaries and their work around the world. Commit to pray for these courageous brothers and sisters in Christ who truly risk everything for the Lord.

Chapter Twelve Notes

CHAPTER THIRTEEN

Aquila and Priscilla—
Believers Who Loved the Church

Paul stayed on in Corinth for some time. Then he left the brothers and sisters and sailed for Syria, accompanied by Priscilla and Aquila. Before he sailed, he had his hair cut off at Cenchreae because of a vow he had taken. They arrived at Ephesus, where Paul left Priscilla and Aquila. He himself went into the synagogue and reasoned with the Jews. When they asked him to spend more time with them, he declined. But as he left, he promised, "I will come back if it is God's will." Then he set sail from Ephesus. When he landed at Caesarea, he went up to Jerusalem and greeted the church and then went down to Antioch.

After spending some time in Antioch, Paul set out from there and traveled from place to place throughout the region of Galatia and Phrygia, strengthening all the disciples.

Meanwhile a Jew named Apollos, a native of Alexandria, came to Ephesus. He was a learned man, with a thorough knowledge of the Scriptures. He had been instructed in the way of the Lord, and he spoke with great fervor and taught about Jesus accurately, though he knew only the baptism of John. He began to speak boldly in the synagogue. When

Priscilla and Aquila heard him, they invited him to their home and explained to him the way of God more adequately.

—Acts 18:18–26

As we've considered ordinary giants in the New Testament, we've compared them to examples of people we look up to in the church today. Not all leaders are visible; some leaders work behind the scenes to inspire greatness in others. Many believers love the church—all of God's people who gather together—and show that love by their actions.

Elaine has led a women's Bible study group for twenty years. A team of guys shows up every Monday to maintain the church grounds. Margie has helped count the offering on Monday mornings for a decade. A couple cleans the church bathrooms on a regular basis. Bill has a cheerful word of greeting for everyone who walks through the doors. Believers who love and serve the church help make it a welcoming place for people from the community to come and meet Jesus.

Two laypeople—a married couple—were tremendously effective in reaching out for their community. They connected with the church and the community in ways that honored God.

Lessons from Aquila and Priscilla

Throughout Paul's ministry, Aquila and Priscilla served as laypeople who did great things for God. Most of us will never be called to be preachers—we'll serve God as laypeople in the church. We have normal jobs, but we also participate in our church.

I may preach at a revival service, but members of the church do the heavy lifting. They prepare a place for people to come and hear the good news about Jesus. In some cases, churches have lay revivals. Those meetings are organized efforts by churches to have laymen speak about their experiences and about how God has changed their lives. Ordinary giants have a tremendous effect on God's kingdom when they share the gospel, formally or informally.

Aquila and Priscilla loved the mission of the church. This couple loved the mission of the church and they had a heart for sharing the love of Jesus with others. When Paul met them, they were living in Corinth (Acts 18:1–2). They left with Paul and sailed with him for Syria, then they stayed on in Ephesus (Acts 18:18–19). Later we find them back in their hometown of Rome, when Paul mentions in his letter "they risked their lives for me" (Romans 16:4). In Ephesus, and again in Rome, they had a church meeting in their home (Acts 18:26; 1 Corinthians 16:19). Priscilla and Aquila loved the mission of the church; they believed wholeheartedly in spreading the good news about Jesus Christ everywhere they went.

What is our mission as Christians? The mission of any church that bears the name of Christ should be to present Jesus Christ as the one and only Savior of the world and invite a watching world to join us. That's our mission! It's not to get involved in every political fight or every social movement, because this year it may be one cause and next year it could be something else.

Our mission is to keep the main thing the main thing, to present Jesus Christ as the one and only Savior. He's the one who comes into our hearts, takes away our sins, gives us the Holy Spirit to walk with us day after day, and promises us eternal life when we die. That's what Christianity is about! It doesn't mean we're to be wallflowers and never speak out on issues, because if good men do nothing, that's a problem. But as Christians, we are to be the light of the world. We're to go out and make a difference: to be husbands with great integrity, wives and mothers who love children and uphold the family unit, children who obey our parents. We're to be honorable people in our communities. Christians are supposed to be different.

The mission of the church is to present Jesus Christ as the way, the truth, and the life, and there's no one like Jesus (John 14:6). It's simple.

Recently, I was asked to go to a home and talk to a couple who were not Christians. They lived in a good part of town, and we sat in their nicely-appointed living room. They said they liked our church. Then we got to the main point: their lives were falling apart. Tears came into the wife's eyes and she said, "We're not happy. We've been running from God for a long time. How do we become Christians?"

I presented the gospel to them and asked if they believed this good news about what Jesus has done for us. They said yes. I believe a lot of people know they're sinners, they know they're not perfect, and they may even know Jesus died on the cross. They're not debating any of that. Perhaps they respect the church and even attend on a regular basis. But they're not Christians. Evangelism asks them to make a decision to receive Christ into their lives. I asked that couple, "Would you like to receive Christ tonight?" and they did.

That's the mission of the church. Priscilla and Aquila understood this:

> Meanwhile, a Jew named Apollos, a native of Alexandria, came to Ephesus. He was a learned man, with a thorough knowledge of the Scriptures. He had been instructed in the way of the Lord, and he spoke with great fervor and taught about Jesus accurately.... He began to speak boldly in the synagogue. When Priscilla and Aquila heard him, they invited him to their home and explained to him the way of God more adequately.
>
> —*Acts 18:24–26*

Priscilla and Aquila helped Paul in his ministry, and they helped Apollos as well.

Aquila and Priscilla loved the message of the church. The message of the church is about Jesus but it's also about love, "because God is love" (1 John 4:8). It's okay for Christians to smile! When I said that recently at church, about ten people told me later, "I wish other people would smile!"

The message of the church is about extending the kindness Jesus Christ offers to people. We can do this through missions but also in the simple things. It doesn't always have to be in a church building; in fact, most of the time, it won't be. It's going to be in the kind acts no one will ever know about. Priscilla and Aquila kindly took Apollos aside to help him with his message and ministry. They remembered and sent greetings to believers they had met in their travels with Paul. They opened their home to believers with welcome and kindness; we read that a church met in their house in more than one place they lived.

When I was in seminary, a kind woman in her mid-eighties wrote me a letter once a month. Most of the time she included a small amount of money that typically helped me afford to buy ice cream. I still remember those small acts of kindness. The message I received from her was one of true affection. Does anyone write letters anymore? We send emails and texts, we connect with people on social media, we send our offerings through online giving—all fine and good, but do we ever spend time writing a note to someone? It's awesome when I receive a note. Write a note this week to thank someone for something or to extend kindness in some way.

Aquila and Priscilla loved the Master of the church. Priscilla and Aquila loved and served Jesus, the Master of the church. We see that in their willingness to set aside their lives for the work of the gospel. They left Corinth to travel with Paul; they opened their home again and again; and they risked their lives for Paul (wouldn't we love to know the rest of *that* story?).

Jesus Christ is our only master. Someone said, "Your church has a nice presence downtown." But it's not *my* church, it's the church of Jesus Christ. He's the Master, the one we get our marching orders from, the one we try to present to the world every day. When we allow Him to work through us, unbelievable things happen.

A group of young people sang at a church gathering.

All of them had troubled backgrounds. Not one of them ever imagined they would sing in a church for Jesus. That's the Master at work.

I heard about a family who had been touched by cancer. Their family and church family rallied around and gave them support. That's the mission and message and the Master of the church working together.

These people were all laypeople. They were common folk who had experienced the love of God, and they loved Him in return. God's not looking for extraordinary people but for ordinary giants who are willing to allow Him to do larger-than-life things through their lives. It's not our abilities, but it's our availability God wants. When we're available to God, our love for the Master, the mission of His church, and His message spills over into love and service for others. He will take the little things we do and turn them into something great for His kingdom.

Walking in Aquila and Priscilla's Footsteps

Jesus spent time in the synagogue—the local church—during His time on earth. One day He observed people bringing their offerings:

> *Jesus sat down opposite the place where the offerings were put and watched the crowd putting their money into the temple treasury. Many rich people threw in large amounts. But a poor widow came and put in two very small copper coins, worth only a few cents.*
>
> *Calling his disciples to him, Jesus said, "Truly I tell you; this poor widow has put more into the treasury than all the*

others. They all gave out of their wealth; but she, out of her
poverty, put in everything—all she had to live on."
Mark 12:41–44

Jesus pointed out she had given all, more than anyone. It's not what we give, it's what we have left. Are we sacrificing everything to love God and others?

Jesus called attention to this ordinary giant as someone the disciples could look up to as a leader. Leaders—laypeople like Aquila and Priscilla and this poor widow—are people who inspire others to greatness, to be better people than they were before. The widow took a risk and gave out of love for God. She trusted Him as the captain of her life.

Aquila and Priscilla gave it all to help the mission, the message, and the Master of the church. When we set everything aside, as Aquila and Priscilla did, out of love for Jesus and others, our lives will never be the same.

WORKBOOK

Chapter Thirteen Questions

Question: Describe a lay couple you have known who have worked together to serve the Lord through the church. What made them a great team? How have they been invaluable to the pastors and/or missionaries they have served alongside?

_____

_____

_____

_____

_____

_____

_____

_____

_____

Question: What are some kind acts that others have done for you that encouraged you in your walk with the Lord? What are some acts of kindness that you are especially gifted or equipped to do? How can you use these to further the ministry of the church?

_____

_____

_____

_____

_____

_____

_____

_____

_____

_____

_____

Question: Why is it important to love the Master of the church more than the church itself? What are the dangers of misplaced loyalty to a pastor, a building, a denomination, or a congregation? How can you evaluate whether you are truly serving the church or the Master of the church?

_____

_____

_____

_____

_____

_____

_____

_____

_____

_____

_____

_____

Action: Take time this week to be a part of ministry with your church. Consider serving in a capacity you have never tried before. Note the laypeople who are serving with you and thank them for their devotion to Christ and His church.

Chapter Thirteen Notes

CHAPTER FOURTEEN

Nicodemus—
The One Who Desired Real Faith

Now there was a Pharisee, a man named Nicodemus who was a member of the Jewish ruling council. He came to Jesus at night and said, "Rabbi, we know that you are a teacher who has come from God. For no one could perform the signs you are doing if God were not with him." Jesus replied, "Very truly I tell you, no one can see the kingdom of God unless they are born again." "How can someone be born when they are old?" Nicodemus asked. "Surely they cannot enter a second time into their mother's womb to be born!" Jesus answered, "Very truly I tell you, no one can enter the kingdom of God unless they are born of water and the Spirit....

For God so loved the world that he gave his one and only Son, that whoever believes in him shall not perish but have eternal life. For God did not send his Son into the world to condemn the world, but to save the world through him. Whoever believes in him is not condemned, but whoever does not believe stands condemned already because they have not believed in the name of God's one and only Son. This is the verdict: Light has come into the world, but people loved darkness instead of light because their deeds were evil.

—John 3:1–5, 16–19

Amber yearns to learn more about Jesus. This isn't always easy, as she often travels on the weekend for her job as a coach in a college women's basketball program. She works long hours at home during the busy season. But Amber always tries to find a church and a small group to attend wherever she lives. She looks forward to meeting with Jesus when she's able to attend worship services. When Amber is on the road, she satisfies her yearning for God by singing worship songs along with the radio. Amber says she yearns to respond to Jesus by doing His work to the fullest capacity He has given her through her profession to further God's kingdom. She responds to God by doing her best and always looking for what God has in store for her next.

Lessons from Nicodemus

Although Nicodemus lived thousands of years ago during the time of Jesus' earthly ministry, he also experienced a yearning for God. He served on the seventy-member Sanhedrin, as one of the religious rulers (John 3:1). No doubt he was one of the wealthiest people in the country. He was curious about anything related to God. He had heard the stories about the man from Nazareth in Galilee named Jesus (Luke 3:2). After hearing so much about Him, Nicodemus decided to meet with Him.

We look up to Nicodemus as an ordinary giant because he wanted to know more—he yearned for God. Because of his position on the ruling council, Nicodemus went to meet Jesus at night (Luke 3:2). But the important thing is that he went. He dared to satisfy his hunger and yearning to know more about God. What do we long for in this life? Are we actively seeking answers to our questions about God?

Nicodemus desired to learn about Jesus. Nicodemus was curious about Jesus, and people today are curious about Him, too. We hear God's name spoken in vain a lot in our culture, but how many times do we hear another deity's name mentioned in vain? We hear the name Jesus, Jesus Christ, or God used as a curse, but no other deities are ridiculed in such a way. There's something about the name of Jesus.

Even though he was part of the Jewish ruling council, the Sanhedrin, and had many things going for him, there was something about Jesus that drew Nicodemus.

I met someone in a hospital who said he'd been watching our broadcasts for ten years but had never been to a church service. He was curious, but he never came to church or believed in Christ. Jesus clarified for Nicodemus it's not enough to be curious; one must take a step of faith and respond.

> *Whoever believes in him is not condemned, but whoever does not believe stands condemned already because they have not believed in the name of God's one and only Son.*
> *—John 3:18*

To respond in faith to Jesus, you must believe in Christ's resurrection and confess Him as Lord of your life (Romans 10:9).

After I took my son to college, I drove his small Mustang home to trade it off. I stopped to get gas, and an older gentleman next to me asked, "You going through a mid-life crisis?" I said no and went inside to pay for the gas. He saw my shirt with the church logo and talked with me for twenty minutes. Right there in the gas station lobby we prayed together. His curiosity led to belief.

Recently, I took my daughter's car to fill it up with gas. I was wearing the same shirt and matching hat with the church logo. A lady ran over and asked, "Brother Harmon, is that you?" She introduced me to her daughter, who was pregnant with twins and needed prayer. Right there next to the gas pumps, I laid hands on her and prayed over her. There's power in prayer, and there's also curiosity about Jesus and all things of God because He is still in the healing business. He still transforms lives. Who knows how that prayer might have touched that young lady and led to a response in her life toward God at a later point?

Pastor and author A. W. Tozer said, "We please Him most not by frantically trying to make ourselves good, but by throwing ourselves into His arms with all our imperfections and believing that He understands everything—and loves us still."[47] That's the message Jesus shared with Nicodemus, "for God so loved the world that he gave his one and only Son, that whoever believes in him shall not perish but have eternal life" (John 3:16).

We're not holy—God is. Nicodemus yearned to learn more about Jesus. He understood Jesus was not just another teacher, and he brought his questions to discover more about who Jesus was (John 3:2, 4, 9).

Nicodemus desired to meet Jesus. Nicodemus set aside his pride, position, and prestige to meet with Jesus. He put it all on the line to meet Jesus. He didn't ask his questions of someone else to satisfy his curiosity; he found a way to meet Jesus in person.

When I had cancer, there wasn't one agnostic that came to me to offer hope. But God in heaven sent His ministering angel, His Holy Spirit; He sent His Word and His church to help me get through a difficult time. We have to put down our pride and come to Jesus as we are.

Kyle Idleman, a pastor in Louisville, Kentucky, said, "God's grace is compelling when explained, but irresistible when experienced."[48] When we experience the grace of God, we know for a fact how good God is. This is what Nicodemus experienced when he met Jesus face to face. Jesus met Nicodemus where he was and told him about the grace of God shown by His mercy and loving-kindness.

Jesus' words in John 3:16 hold the key to the kingdom of heaven. We believe this verse contains the true gospel—good news—of Jesus Christ, for every person in the entire world: anyone can have eternal life with God. God can save anyone. He doesn't want anyone to perish but for all to come to repentance. God knows who will make the choice to believe in Him, but He *desires* everyone would be saved.

I once preached a revival service in an old church in a coal community in Kentucky. The church sat right on the main road and had windows of clear glass. The second day of the revival, I noticed a young man walking by. He stayed and listened for five minutes before leaving. The next day he stayed about ten minutes. When I saw him on the last night of the revival, I hoped he would stay fifteen minutes. To my joy, he came in and sat on the back row and listened to every word of my sermon.

During the last stanza of the invitation hymn, this young man walked down the aisle and gave his heart to Christ. The whole church felt a sense of revival because he was a well-known leader of the young people in the community. That young man met Jesus, and it made a difference in his life. Today, he's active in a church in another city. With God, all things are possible! He can take us places we can't even believe.

Nicodemus desired to respond to Jesus. Nicodemus wanted to understand Jesus' teaching for himself. He kept asking questions to dig deeper into the meaning of Jesus' words. How do we know Nicodemus responded to Jesus? After Jesus' death, Joseph of Arimathea, a secret disciple of Jesus, asked Pilate for Jesus' body. "He was accompanied by Nicodemus, the man who earlier had visited Jesus at night" (John 19:39).

In his initial conversation with Jesus, Nicodemus discovered that being born again is the only acceptable response to Christ, rather than book knowledge. As we discussed this passage one day in seminary, we read Jesus' words in John 3:3: "...no one can see the kingdom of God unless they are born again." One of the students said, "Professor, do you think born-again Christians are the only Christians?" Bewildered, the professor said, "Are there any other type of Christians? I think not. This verse says you have to be born again."

The church in America today tries to de-emphasize Scripture and instead emphasize experience. Whatever our personal experience or preferences, we all become a Christian the same way. Christians are people who have received Jesus Christ as their Lord and Savior, who have received the gift of His blood shed on the cross for forgiveness of their sins (Romans 10:9–10; Hebrews 9:22). They once were dead in their sins, but now they're alive in Christ Jesus (Ephesians 2:1–5), and His forgiveness has been applied to their hearts. All of us who have called on the name of Jesus as our Savior and Lord are born again (Romans 10:9).

Jesus makes it clear to Nicodemus that he, as a member of the Jewish ruling council, was not a judge of humanity's sinfulness—and neither are we, for that matter. Our witness of who Jesus is and what He has done should point only to God's grace. We often quote John 3:16 and stop before we get to verse 17: "For God did not send his Son into the world to condemn the world, but to save the world through him." Many of us want to be in the judging business, not the witnessing business. It's easy to place ourselves on a pedestal and say, "People should be more like me," or, "That person's a sinner and I'm not."

It's easy to judge others and to think we're right about everything. I don't think we understand the power of our words. We represent the King of kings. The most important thing is to witness—to tell others—about the magnificent and amazing grace of Jesus Christ. I want the world to know and respond to Christ and His forgiveness!

Nicodemus yearned to know more about Jesus, and he responded to Jesus. Later in John's account, we read that Nicodemus, still part of the Sanhedrin, spoke in defense of Jesus, according to their own law (John 7:50–51).[49] The last time we encounter Nicodemus in the gospel story, he assists Joseph of Arimathea with the burial of Jesus. We don't know who may have witnessed this, but we know it no longer mattered to those two secret disciples. Joseph asked Pilate publicly for the body, and Nicodemus brought a tribute fit for a king for all to see.[50]

Walking in Nicodemus' Footsteps

We look to Nicodemus as an ordinary giant because of his humanity: he had fears, doubts, and obligations that could have kept him from Jesus. But he had enough curiosity, desire, and longing for things of God to take a risk and investigate. Learning more about Jesus and what it means to be born again often requires us to put aside our intellect and position in order to move to a deeper understanding of and relationship with Christ.

Nicodemus didn't settle for what others said about Jesus; he yearned to know for himself. As a rational thinker and leader, he had already concluded God must have sent Jesus (John 3:2). Nicodemus made the effort to meet Jesus in person, to ask questions to learn more about Jesus, and to consider what he learned and apply it to his life. He wrestled with the answers Jesus gave to his questions and ultimately turned his life over to Jesus as the leader and Lord of his life.

WORKBOOK

Chapter Fourteen Questions

Question: Do you have a hunger and a yearning to know more about God and to know God Himself? How is this yearning manifested in your life? How does a true hunger for God differ from mere curiosity about Him?

_____

_____

_____

_____

_____

_____

_____

_____

_____

_____

Question: What is your story of meeting Jesus face to face—that is, experiencing His love in a personal way and being born again, rather than just acquiring information about Him? What would you say to a person who claims to be a Christian but has never had a personal encounter with God's grace and forgiveness?

_____

_____

_____

_____

_____

_____

_____

_____

_____

_____

_____

Question: Why do you think Nicodemus went from being a secret disciple to openly supporting Jesus? When have you been tempted to hide your faith? What has given you boldness in talking about the Lord?

_____

_____

_____

_____

_____

_____

_____

_____

_____

_____

_____

_____

Action: Memorize John 3:16–21. There are many books and sermons on John 3:16. Read or listen to one as part of your study of Nicodemus and this passage.

Chapter Fourteen Notes

_____

_____

_____

_____

_____

_____

_____

_____

_____

_____

_____

_____

_____

_____

_____

_____

_____

_____

_____

CHAPTER FIFTEEN

Joseph—A Father of Character

This is how the birth of Jesus the Messiah came about: His mother Mary was pledged to be married to Joseph, but before they came together, she was found to be pregnant through the Holy Spirit. Because Joseph her husband was faithful to the law, and yet did not want to expose her to public disgrace, he had in mind to divorce her quietly.

But after he had considered this, an angel of the Lord appeared to him in a dream and said, "Joseph son of David, do not be afraid to take Mary home as your wife, because what is conceived in her is from the Holy Spirit. She will give birth to a son, and you are to give him the name Jesus, because he will save his people from their sins."

All this took place to fulfill what the Lord had said through the prophet: "The virgin will conceive and give birth to a son, and they will call him Immanuel" (which means "God with us").

When Joseph woke up, he did what the angel of the Lord had commanded him and took Mary home as his wife. But he did not consummate their marriage until she gave birth to a son. And he gave him the name Jesus.

—Matthew 1:18–25

Ordinary giants are people of character; we look up to them. Character is the person you are when no one else is looking. God is looking for people of character to guide others to Him. Are we people of character?

Joseph was the earthly father of Jesus—a father with character, someone I've always looked up to and admired. He had a hard road to travel, but he gently led Mary as they followed God's will for their lives.

When I think about dads in the church, I see a real problem today. Some won't like my statement: men are absent in the church. For the most part, churches have become feminized. I'm all for allowing women to have roles in ministry, but men, you've let the Lord down. More than that, you've let your family down.

Let's look at troubling statistics in our country. According to a 2010 census, 33 percent of children in the United States live absent their biological father. A census from 2012 found that among children who are part of the post-war generation, 87.7 percent grew up with both biological parents who were married to each other. Today, only 68.1 percent will spend their entire childhoods in an intact family.[51] These statistics cross racial and socio-economics lines, as we see substantial percentages of all children living absent from their biological fathers.

Where are the dads in the church? Where are the young men learning the things of God? As a coach, dad, and pastor, I believe I have enough credibility to say too many parents are more interested in ensuring their son or daughter makes the team rather than makes the kingdom, or gets into an Ivy League school rather than gets right with Jesus Christ. Above all, make sure your children know Christ as

Lord and Savior. We need to understand the consequences. This is eternal. Games are won and lost, teams are formed and changed, but the kingdom is forever.

At a recent youth service, I was proud to see young men on stage and involved in the service. We need to have men working in the nursery—they need men's faces there. We need men in the children's area. Some of these kids never see a male figure in their lives. People ask, how can I serve God? Work with children. They rarely see men anymore, and the men they do see are often in and out. It's easier to have a child than to be a father.

Lessons from Joseph

Joseph wasn't an absentee father. He was a man of character. He met Mary and loved her, but then something strange and troubling took place. Seemingly out of the blue, God the Father chose to impregnate Joseph's fiancée, Mary, to carry Jesus. When Joseph found out, what was he to do? His friends probably said, "She's with child by someone else. You need to put her away." Matthew records Joseph's initial response: "Because Joseph her husband was faithful to the law, and yet did not want to expose her to public disgrace, he had in mind to divorce her quietly" (Matthew 1:19).

This isn't the end of Joseph's story—it's only the beginning. The rest of his story provides clear examples for all of us to follow in one way or another, whether or not we are a father or head of household. God calls us, as people of character, to steer our ships straight in a storm and lead others to Him.

Joseph protected his family. Most dads do a great job protecting their families from outside influences, physical violence, etc. Fathers naturally protect their families. I recall going to amusement parks with my kids on vacations. I was always concerned they'd be vulnerable in such large crowds; for example, they might have bad people around them when they took a bathroom break. We all typically look for ways to protect our children, brothers and sisters, parents—whichever family members we're with.

Joseph's initial instinct in reaction to Mary's news was to divorce her quietly, but another strange event took place:

> After he had considered this, an angel of the Lord appeared to him in a dream and said, "Joseph son of David, do not be afraid to take Mary home as your wife, because what is conceived in her is from the Holy Spirit." ... When Joseph woke up, he did what the angel of the Lord had commanded him and took Mary home as his wife.
> **—Matthew 1:20, 24**

God sent Joseph an angel to tell him it was okay to continue with his original plans. Joseph's friends may have counseled him to get rid of her, but he knew God was going to do something amazing.

Joseph not only protected his family later, but he also protected the sanctity of marriage from the outset. Marriage takes work. There are people in our church who've been married over sixty-five years. Think about that! I always ask the same question: how do you do it? My favorite answer came from Clarence, a tax collector and city clerk for many years. He said, "In addition to loving somebody, you've got to like them." There will be good days and bad days as a husband or as a wife, but together, it's something special.

Joseph protected his family, and we need to protect ours, whether we are making sure others don't talk down about our spouses, safeguarding our families from violence, or monitoring what our kids listen to or watch on all their devices.

Tony Evans, the great Texan preacher, said, "[Men,] we are not put in the family to help, but to lead—and to lead well."[52] Dads are to be leaders in their homes. Often—nearly three-quarters of the time—when a husband and father makes a decision for Christ, his family will follow.[53] Parents can't become Christians *for* their sons or daughters, but often their children will follow in their footsteps after seeing their godly examples

Joseph was present for his family. People sometimes try to explain away their absenteeism: "I may not give them quantity, but I give them quality time." What do kids want? Quantity. They want and deserve a lot of our time. Sometimes, our jobs take us away and we aren't able to be with our children, but we all have choices.

I had to make a decision. I had a wonderful position with an organization and traveled all around the country, but when it came to raising my family, I sensed the Lord distinctly saying, "Get off the road, stay at home, and invest in your family." I made that choice, and other parents will have to make choices, too.

Find ways to do things you like to do together, such as

taking your children fishing or enjoying activities they enjoy. My daughter, Madison, is a talented artist and enjoys musicals and theater. In an effort to stay connected to her, we enjoy father-daughter evenings together seeing Broadway musicals and theatrical interpretations. She has taught me so much about this world of the arts! Be present in their lives, no matter the time it takes.

Joseph had a carpenter's shop in Nazareth (Matthew 13:55) and may have done stonework as well as woodwork. He used his hands and Jesus grew up using His hands. Jesus was a skilled carpenter as well as the Messiah (Mark 6:3)! Joseph was present in His life.

It's interesting that when twelve-year-old Jesus went to the temple with his parents, which was the custom for Jewish families, they lost Jesus—He stayed behind at the temple. Joseph didn't tell Mary, "You go on to Jerusalem for the Feast, and I'll meet you when you come back." No, Joseph went to the Feast and took his family with him. I like it when dads don't just drop off their families at church but, instead, get out of the car, walk with them into church, and lead them in worship. It's called being the spiritual leader of the home.

Joseph was present, as dads need to be present in their sons' and daughters' lives. Influence them, pray with them, pray over them, and guide them as the Lord directs.

Joseph provided for his family. He provided financially and with spiritual guidance he received from the Lord (Matthew 2:13–23). He provided skills for Jesus and also income for the family. I encourage dads not to be driven by money but, at the same time, to take care of the family. Live by example the principle that everything belongs to

God: as we give to Him our tithes and offerings, He often shows us His gracious provision as our heavenly Father.

Paul counseled his *son in the faith*, Timothy, on this matter, "Anyone who does not provide for their relatives, and especially for their own household, has denied the faith and is worse than an unbeliever" (1 Timothy 5:8). Kevin DeYoung, who is an author, pastor, and board chairman of The Gospel Coalition, expands on this thought for believers today:[54]

> Most Christian husbands and fathers recognized the need to provide for their families ... Even as this is true in the physical realm, so it is true in the spiritual. By all means, bring home the bacon! But don't stop there. Practice consistent and regular family worship. Lead your family in reading the scriptures, praying, and singing. In joy, take your family to church each week, engage your family in the ministry of the church, pursue hospitality by inviting others to your home, pray with and for your wife and children. Don't think your job is done by putting a roof over their heads, clothes on their backs, and food in their stomachs [because] they need your provision in the spiritual realm as well.

Walking in Joseph's Footsteps

Joseph provided for and was present with his family physically and spiritually. We need more men of character like Joseph. He was a real giant in the way he protected, was present, and provided for Jesus during His early life. God spoke through the angels to guide Joseph's path, and Joseph was willing to receive the direction from God. Are we?

Single moms may find themselves in a similar position as head of their family. Perhaps a husband left and it was completely his choice. These women take on the role of leading their families. God will provide the strength and character they need, if they ask. It might be an unfortunate situation, but we can't go back and unscramble the egg. Don't dwell on the guilt of the past. Start today and say, "I'm going to do the best I can." Seek God's guidance on how to become an ordinary giant for Him in your family.

As parents, we often realize we've made mistakes, but God offers hope. It's never too late to ask God to forgive us and guide us. Our society needs men to be leaders in the church, in their homes, and in the community. Women are also involved in the important tasks of protecting, providing for, and being present with their families. But where are the men?

I'm a dad who has been involved with my children's activities, and all those things take time. I'm happy to do it; it's been a joy. As I write this, my son is moving to the University of Kentucky to begin college, yet my wife and I remember the first day we held him in our arms. We realize this is now the next step for him into adulthood, and we want the best for him. In the same way parents want the best for their sons and daughters, our heavenly Father wants the best for us. He wants us to follow Him.

If more men stood up as ordinary giants—Christian examples and leaders for their families and communities— imagine how different our society might be.

Chapter Fifteen Questions

Question: When you hear the phrase *person of character*, what qualities come to mind? Looking at Scripture, what do you consider the most important character qualities that a Christian should have in his or her life?

_____

_____

_____

_____

_____

_____

_____

_____

_____

_____

_____

Question: In what ways do you see a lack of male leadership in the church and the culture affecting young people? Who are some men of character and conviction whom you see leading their families? How are they demonstrating protection, presence, and provision?

_____

_____

_____

_____

_____

_____

_____

_____

_____

_____

_____

Question: What are some ways that protection, presence, and provision extend beyond just the tangible and physical to the spiritual realm as well?

_____

_____

_____

_____

_____

_____

_____

_____

_____

_____

_____

_____

Action: If you are a husband and/or father, look at the three areas of protection, presence, and provision. In which area do you need to grow? Set a goal for a practical way you will grow in that area, and ask a Christian friend to keep you accountable.

If you are not a husband and/or father, take time this week to thank someone who is fulfilling those roles with conviction and integrity. This could be a family member, your pastor, or any man in the church who is leading and loving his family well.

Chapter Fifteen Notes

CHAPTER SIXTEEN

Mary—A Devoted Mother

And Mary said:

*"My soul glorifies the Lord and my spirit rejoices in God my
Savior, for he has been mindful of the humble state of his
servant. From now on all generations will call me blessed,
for the Mighty One has done great things for me—holy is
his name. His mercy extends to those who fear him, from
generation to generation. He has performed mighty deeds
with his arm; he has scattered those who are proud in their
inmost thoughts. He has brought down rulers from their
thrones but has lifted up the humble. He has filled the hungry with good things but has sent the rich away empty. He
has helped his servant Israel, remembering to be merciful
to Abraham and his descendants forever, just as he promised our ancestors." Mary stayed with Elizabeth for about
three months and then returned home.*
—Luke 1:46–56

I love my mother, and she has had a tremendous influence on my life. She took me to church with her every
week—Sunday mornings, Sunday evenings, and Wednes-
day nights. She was my Sunday school teacher for a
season. That made an impact! When our kids are going

through the program at church, it's in our—and their—best interests to volunteer in some way. We can teach, be an assistant, chaperone, drive the bus, or go to youth camp. Ordinary giants help with these everyday tasks that make a difference. Our kids like having us around, even if at times they act like they don't. We can be the first mate, acting under the command of God as our captain to carry out His orders—in this case, by pointing our children to God and teaching them to obey all His commands.

God's command to all of us is to obey and honor our parents (Exodus 20:12; Ephesians 6:1–2). We are to respect them, not only during our growing up years but all throughout their lives as well. We'll never regret spending extra time with our parents. While coaching eighth-grade athletes in middle school, I'd hear various comments from the boys: "My mom's not going to be here," "My mom can't be here," or "I don't want my mom here." Lots of different emotions were expressed. I believe the healthiest families are the ones with a strong bond between mother and child.

Lessons from Mary

One of the most significant people in all of the New Testament was Jesus' mother, Mary. Her song in Luke 1:46–56 is known as the Magnificat, based on the first word of its first line in Latin: "My soul magnifies the Lord" (Luke 1:46 ESV).[55] In this passage, Mary shares her commitment not only to becoming the mother of Jesus, but also to acknowledging Jesus as the Savior of the world.

God the Father chose one person, of all the millions of people who had been born and would be born, to bear His Son. One person to carry the seed of the Savior. He chose this young woman named Mary. She was a virtuous, godly woman with high morals, yet not well-known.

Mary's hymn of praise begins, "My soul glorifies the Lord and my spirit rejoices in God my Savior, for he has been mindful of the humble state of his servant" (Luke 1:46–48). She praises God for His mercy in the presence of her relative Elizabeth. It's not clear exactly when the Holy Spirit impregnated Mary with Jesus (Luke 1:35), although it may have been before she arrived at Elizabeth's house, since Elizabeth says, "Blessed are you among women, and blessed is the child you will bear! But why am I so favored, that the mother of my Lord should come to me?" (Luke 1:42–43). Even though Mary was pledged to be married to Joseph, she had known no man. Mary was bewildered, but she said, "I am the Lord's servant," and added, "May your word to me be fulfilled" (Luke 1:38). Willing to be a humble servant of God, Mary could be trusted.

Mary had a profound spiritual sensitivity. Mary's song is in part an outpouring of her inner thoughts regarding this amazing turn of events in her life. Mary accepted the words of the angel. She traveled to spend time with Elizabeth, who may have served as a mentor. After she returned home, Mary willingly followed Joseph in obedience to the guidance he also had received from God. All of this shows Mary was someone who thought deeply about the things of God. Why did God choose her, out of all the people in the world? Her only response was submission and praise: "May your word to me be fulfilled" (Luke 1:38), and, "My soul glorifies the Lord and my spirit rejoices in God my Savior" (Luke 1:46).

Mary realized her child wasn't an ordinary baby—He was God and a personal Savior. Of all the things mothers might pray about, such as their children's health and well-being, spiritual sensitivity is the most significant. When God begins to do things in a mother's life, He shares His Word. When a mother sees things she's never seen before, and when God speaks through a mother's prayers and asks her to do things, He's calling her to be sensitive. Mary was sensitive to the Holy Spirit, and she loved the Lord.

Some mother will give birth to the next Billy Graham or the next great missionary. There are godly mothers who are right now raising great future leaders of the church, pastors, and teachers. Mothers raise our future governors and mayors. Mothers have tremendous influence.

This influence begins as we teach our children the ways of God: prayer, Bible study, church attendance, giving to God, and witnessing to tell others what God has done. King Solomon said, "Start children off on the way they should go, and even when they are old they will not turn from it" (Proverbs 22:6). It's our job to help our children understand what it means to be a Christian and to encourage them to keep themselves pure from the world. Mary, along with Joseph, instructed Jesus, protected Him, and provided an environment in which "Jesus grew in wisdom and stature, and in favor with God and man" (Luke 2:52).

Jesus was fully God here on earth, but Mary was chosen by the heavenly Father to give birth to Jesus the Son and to participate in His humanity. That's a mystery almost too profound to fathom. Why would God choose one particular person to bear the Son of Man? God chooses all mothers to carry the seeds of their children. He entrusts the seed of each individual human being to a mother to care for and nurture that soul and to guide that person back to God, the heavenly Father. Any mother of identical twins can testify God creates each person as a unique individual—there are differences. God gave Mary the blessing of spiritual sensitivity, and He offers it to all mothers who seek Him.

Mary was prepared to be used by God. Success is often described as the point when preparation meets opportunity. When we're prepared and willing and able to do whatever God calls us to do, we're going to have spiritual success. Jesus described it this way: "His master replied, 'Well done, good and faithful servant! You have been faithful with a few things; I will put you in charge of many things'" (Matthew 25:21). When we do what God has called us to do in the small things, He may ask us to do something big. Faithful mothers show they are prepared to be used by God in special ways.

Sometimes God's process of preparing us to do something in particular lasts many years before He calls us at just the right time. After a lifetime of following and serving Jesus, He called Mary to a different way of serving Him:

Near the cross of Jesus stood his mother.... When Jesus saw his mother there, and the disciple whom he loved standing nearby, he said to her, "Woman, here is your son," and to the disciple, "Here is your mother." From that time on, this disciple took her into his home

—John 19:25–27

Jesus prepared Mary for His death and resurrection, and He prepared His disciples, as their community became the early church, caring for one another while spreading the good news about Jesus. Mary was not only spiritually sensitive, but she was also prepared to be used by the Father in new and wonderful ways. God prepares us for His work if we are willing.

Andy Stanley, an Atlanta preacher, said, "Your greatest contribution to the kingdom of God may not be something you do, but someone you raise."[56] This applies to any parents. I'm appreciative of adoptive parents— those who see a need, reach out, and take in one whom God has prepared for them. Whether or not an adoption is planned, it can become a significant opportunity. Thank you, adoptive moms and dads. You are important to God's kingdom. In many cases, you're taking in children who would otherwise have no home.

Mothers don't always have to be right; most of all, they just need to be there. In his devotional *Experiencing God Day by Day*, Richard Blackaby said, "You may not realize it, but your life has the potential to bless everyone you encounter."[57] When I was growing up, I didn't like school food. Mom packed my lunch. My mother's the best cook in the world! She did a lot with a little. Mom did something no other parent did at the time: she would write, "I love you," on the waxed paper in which she folded my sandwich. It embarrassed me, but looking back, I realize how special that gesture was.

Are we preparing our children to be used by God? The first step is to help our children be spiritually sensitive to His leading by praying for them. It's important to pray with our children and to ask them to pray with us.

Mary recognized and professed her commitment to Jesus. Mary was the mother of Jesus, but she acknowledged He was God. Before He was even born, she said, "My spirit rejoices in God my Savior" (Luke 1:47). In her article "Three Things You Didn't Know About Jesus," Kristine Brown wrote of Mary, "Her knowledge of God's promise to send a Savior for His people showed through her worship."[58] Great mothers acknowledge Jesus is God in front of their children. Those who have a profound impact on children tell them about the God who made us, gives us salvation, and gives us hope.

In a day and age when there's so much out there to grab our kids' attention, spiritually and otherwise, we need to point them to God. If we stand firm for Jesus, He will stand firm for us. Pastor Adrian Rogers said, "Faith believes in spite of the circumstances and acts in spite of the consequences."[59] Mary's faith stood firm as she and Joseph followed God's lead and took Jesus to Egypt (Matthew 2:13). They did not foresee these circumstances as part of raising a child, and I'm sure there were consequences to leaving their home country for a time. They had to stand firm for God in a foreign land and remain committed to raising Jesus in their faith. Mary and Joseph didn't turn away from God in hard times; when they returned home, they took Jesus to the temple according to the Jewish custom (Luke 2:41–42).

As Jesus was dying on the cross, He saw His mother and took care of her (John 19:25–27), and He'll take care of every mother who calls on the name of the Lord. He is a good God. He wants every mom to be spiritually sensitive, like Mary. Jesus wants every mom to be prepared to do great things for Him, to profess Christ, and to make sure her household does the same. Every mom needs to be a Christian. That's pretty exclusive, but it's what Jesus taught: "I am the way and the truth and the life. No one comes to the Father except through me" (John 14:6). Acknowledging Jesus as Lord and Savior and committing our lives to Him is the only way we can walk with Him through the tough job of raising children.

Walking in Mary's Footsteps

Moms have the hardest job in the world. I tried to keep track of my wife Rachael's schedule this week—it would have been impossible for the average person to navigate everything on our family calendar! But she does it for our family, for our kids.

The best gift children can give their moms is to give their hearts to Jesus and become Christians; it's a blessing to others, including their parents. The greatest decision families can make is to find a church to attend together, worship together, and get involved.

Devoted mothers set examples for their children by being devoted to God first. Such mothers of godly character are spiritually sensitive and willing to follow God's leading. They walk with God and are open to His Spirit. This prepares them to be used by God for His purposes. The first step in becoming a people of godly character is to recognize Jesus as Lord and Savior and commit our hearts and lives to Him.

Ordinary giants recognize they can't go through life on their own; they need God. We look up to people whose spiritual sensitivity and commitment to Jesus enables them to honor and respect their parents, even if their mom or dad aren't Christians. These people are leaders for God because they are willing to be used by God—perhaps as a blessing in a mom or dad's life or to bring one or both parents to Jesus. Mary's sensitivity and openness to God's work in her life—even when she didn't understand it all— is a powerful example for us as we commit to Jesus as our Lord and Savior.

Chapter Sixteen Questions

Question: What are some markers of spiritual sensitivity, compared to a calloused or hardened heart toward God? Which would you say characterizes you? How do you know?

_____

_____

_____

_____

_____

_____

_____

_____

_____

_____

Question: In what ways has God prepared you for the work or circumstances to which He has called you, and how might He be preparing you now for something He has in your future? How can you encourage your children (or young people in your church) in embracing rather than circumventing God's seasons of preparation in their lives?

_____

_____

_____

_____

_____

_____

_____

_____

_____

_____

_____

Question: If you are a parent, what are your desires and prayers for your child(ren)? Are you investing at least as much time in their spiritual development as in their education, social life, and hobbies/athletics? What specific things are you doing to influence them to love God and be used by Him?

If you are not a parent, or if your children are grown, who are some children God has placed in your sphere of influence, and how are you using that influence for Him?

_____

_____

_____

_____

_____

_____

_____

_____

_____

_____

_____

_____

Action: Read and study Mary's Magnificat in Luke 1. Remember that this beautiful praise was offered *before* Jesus' birth and likely before Mary knew how everything would work out regarding her marriage to Joseph. It was a time when she naturally might have felt anxious or frightened about the assignment she had accepted. Write out your own prayer of praise to God. Focus on the joy of belonging to Him and serving Him as opposed to the uncertainties and difficulties you face.

Chapter Sixteen Notes

CHAPTER SEVENTEEN

People of Excellence

Finally, brothers and sisters, whatever is true, whatever is noble, whatever is right, whatever is pure, whatever is lovely, whatever is admirable—if anything is excellent or praiseworthy—think about such things. Whatever you have learned or received or heard from me, or seen in me— put it into practice. And the God of peace will be with you.
—***Philippians 4:8–9***

Soon after Bryan and Michelle married, Bryan got a job in a different city and they moved. They wanted to find a church home that would be the best fit for them. How would they determine this? Bryan and Michelle believe God calls His people to proclaim His Word, to make more and better disciples, and to serve Him with all their hearts—and to do all these things with excellence out of reverence for God. Bryan researched online and read the statement of faith for several churches in the area. As they visited each church, they evaluated their worship experience through their filters of excellence.

Lessons from Ordinary Giants

Jesus didn't use the word *excellence* in His ministry, and He called ordinary people to follow Him; He accepted people as they were. But He poured His heart, soul, and life into His disciples. He saw the potential in each of His followers to do great things for God's kingdom. God knows that people like the disciples can change the world. That's His plan. During His time here on earth, Jesus didn't have an elaborate strategy. He invested three years with a group of guys, and they went out to tell the whole world about Jesus. He showed what it looked like to spend time with a handful of people, disciple them, pour into them, and have it result in great success in building God's kingdom.

Jesus loved His followers and taught them His ways. At the right time, everyone would see He would be raised from the dead—that was part of the discipleship strategy for the twelve disciples. One of the twelve, Judas Iscariot, rejected and betrayed Jesus (Matthew 27:3). Judas' example reminds us we can say all the right things and still not believe in our hearts. We all say some wrong things from time to time, but Jesus looks through and sees our true hearts (1 Samuel 16:7). All of us who believe have the potential to serve. Every church—and a church is only the sum of its people—can do great things for God's kingdom if the people follow Jesus Christ.

As a pastor, I've heard people ask, "What could I possibly do for God? I have no outstanding talents or abilities." In God's eyes, there are no insignificant people. Every person is important in His kingdom. What matters is doing what God calls us to do, being a witness of what He has done for us, and serving God Almighty. Every Christian who shares the gospel—the good news about Jesus Christ—plays an important role.

What does it mean to be people who serve God with excellence? I've got a clue for you—it has nothing to do with our choice of music or style of worship! It has nothing to do with which Bible version we use, unless it's not a reputable translation. It doesn't matter what clothes we wear. Our role in preaching the gospel has everything to do with one person, Jesus Christ.

Ordinary giants proclaim the gospel with excellence. After I finished my doctorate, I was involved in a program that took me to several great churches. Each congregation had the same basic tenet: they pursued excellence. They wanted the people who attended their services to have an excellent experience, but even more, they made sure to preach the gospel with excellence.

The apostles encouraged believers to put God first and give Him their best. We are called to focus our thoughts on excellence: "…whatever is true, whatever is noble, whatever is right, whatever is pure, whatever is lovely, whatever is admirable—if anything is excellent or praiseworthy—think about such things" (Philippians 4:8). Jesus Christ is our living example of excellence.

The gospel of Jesus Christ is true, right, excellent, and definitely praiseworthy! If we get things wrong here, nothing else will go right. Proclaim the gospel with excellence. I hope each person can use the Bible to show a lost soul how to become a Christian. Many of us can't; we don't know where to start. We need to learn the basics, how to witness, how to tell people what Jesus Christ has done. It's possible to share the good news about Jesus using only one book of the Bible:

- "For all have sinned and fall short of the glory of God." (Romans 3:23)

- "For the wages of sin is death, but the gift of God is eternal life in Christ Jesus our Lord." (Romans 6:23)

- "But God demonstrates His own love for us in this: While we were still sinners, Christ died for us." (Romans 5:8)

- "Everyone who calls on the name of the Lord will be saved." (Romans 10:13)

We proclaim the gospel with excellence when we take the time to memorize Bible verses that explain what Jesus did. Like Paul, we shouldn't be "ashamed of the gospel, because it is the power of God that brings salvation to everyone who believes: first to the Jew, then to the Gentile" (Romans 1:16). We must rely fully on God's Word, not "with wisdom and eloquence, lest the cross of Christ be emptied of its power" (1 Corinthians 1:17).

Preaching the gospel with excellence happens when we set ourselves aside and put God first. It's all about Jesus Christ and none other. Excellence proclaims His is the *only* gospel (Galatians 1:6–7, Philippians 1:18). As we read in Acts, we discover the apostles were great preachers of the gospel. We need to learn how to proclaim the gospel with excellence—to tell people about the Lord.

A couple of years ago, I was coaching at the state basketball tournament in Lexington when a couple of athletes, twins I'd met previously, came up to me saying, "We know you; you're the preacher who comes to our church." They had both become saved and were serving as youth leaders. Proclaiming the gospel is about multiplying believers for God's kingdom.

We proclaim the gospel when we tell other people how we became a Christian and about what Jesus did for us all. Then we move forward to live for Him as a disciple.

Ordinary giants disciple people with excellence. Jesus commands His disciples (then and now) to "go and make disciples of all nations, baptizing them in the name of the Father and of the Son and of the Holy Spirit, and teaching them to obey everything I have commanded you. And surely I am with you always, to the very end of the age" (Matthew 28:19–20). We are people of excellence when we disciple people well. Some churches state it this way: make *more* and *better* disciples.

We rely on the foundation of God's Word to proclaim the gospel, and we can't be a serious Christian who disciples others with excellence if we don't open our Bibles. In this day and age, we have no excuse. We can use an app on a phone to read a passage at any time. This allows us to have the Bible handy at all times. But it's also good to carry our Bibles to church—and possibly other places, too. A physical book reminds us God's Word is a sword (Hebrews 4:12), an offensive weapon, to use in difficult times.

Disciples of Jesus listen to and obey His Word. As we

pray and study, the Holy Spirit teaches us (John 14:23, 26) and helps us understand how to live as disciples. Jesus' disciples follow His teachings and draw others to Christ. We use words to proclaim Christ, but our lives also become witnesses of God at work in us through the Holy Spirit.

Recently, I went to a local restaurant and the hostess greeted me. She said, "I come to your church; I sit up in the balcony." A few minutes later, I was praying with her because some things were happening in her life. We never know where we're going to meet fellow Christians or where we can be display Jesus' love to non-believers.

We draw others to become disciples when we live out what Jesus taught. In practical terms, this might mean leaving a larger than normal tip for a server. It means treating people with kindness and gentleness.

Christians who disciple others with excellence understand they also need to continue to grow as disciples. They find ways to study the Bible and interact with fellow believers by getting into small groups, for example. Once you become involved in a small group or Sunday school class, the chances you will continue walking with God as a disciple are much greater (Hebrews 10:25). Participating in your local church—in Sunday school, a small group, choir, serving in some way—increases your accountability. When we become better disciples, we can disciple others with excellence.

Ordinary giants serve the Lord with excellence. It's one thing to preach the gospel and to disciple other people, but it's another thing to serve. I've served by preaching and leading—that's what God called me to do—but He calls each of us to serve in different ways. It may be on stage or in other public ways, or it may be behind the scenes. What makes our service excellent is our mindset: "...whatever you do, do it all for the glory of God" (1 Corinthians 10:31). And "have the same mindset as Christ Jesus: who, being in very nature God, did not consider equality with God something to be used to his own advantage; rather, he made himself nothing by taking the very nature of a servant, being made in human likeness" (Philippians 2:5–7). We serve with excellence when we think of others and serve them with love.

Why should we serve in the church? It helps us connect with God and with others. When I talk with people from our church who have gone on mission trips, I love hearing how they connected with the Lord. They got to know fellow believers as well. Service matters because we'll see Jesus face to face one day. Paul mentored Timothy, a young pastor, with these words, "Those who have served well gain an excellent standing and great assurance in their faith in Christ Jesus" (1 Timothy 3:13).

Many Christians I talk with understand they're going to heaven one day. Their attitude might be, "If I can get to heaven, through the gates, that's the main thing." But if we love Jesus, don't we want something to give back to Him? I'd like to be able to say, "Lord, you gave me these opportunities, and here is the result." I want to give something back to God since He's done so much for me.

Many serve the Lord with excellence and proclaim the gospel. Because of God's grace, when I get to heaven, I'm going to think of those people. I'm going to remember Brother Walker, a preacher I heard when I was a kid and walked down the aisle to kneel at an altar and give my life to Jesus. I'm grateful for nursery workers who pour time and love into kids. I thank God for youth leaders who take teens to camp. They are paving the way for countless young people to come to Christ.

Serving with excellence is placing others first (Philippians 2:3) and doing the things no one else is doing. It may look like cleaning the bathrooms at your church, visiting nursing homes, or going above and beyond what's expected of you at work. We are called to serve the Lord with excellence.

The apostles served with excellence after they experienced the truth of Jesus' death and resurrection. We've read how some of the ordinary giants in the New Testament turned away from Jesus and then came back. Thomas was discouraged, but he came back and gathered with the other disciples and was part of exciting things that happened in the early church. John Mark quit at one point but later returned to mission work with Barnabas. Peter took his eyes off Jesus, but then he called out to Jesus in faith and later became a zealous preacher. He preached so passionately the gates of hell did not destroy him. Satan tried to destroy Peter, but Peter kept on preaching.

Satan wants us—our gospel message, our discipleship, our service—destroyed. It's as if Christians wear a big target. He doesn't want us to succeed in anything. When we have Jesus Christ, we are winners—don't ever forget that. Jesus Christ rose victorious from the grave, ascended back to God the Father, and one day He's coming back for His bride, the church. He wants to find us engaged with all our hearts, proclaiming the gospel, discipling others, and serving the Lord, all with excellence. This is why Jesus came! He wants us to be part of His church. Don't be afraid to serve Him.

We never know who's watching our lives. Rachael and I were in a nice restaurant celebrating our anniversary not long ago. Before our meal, we bowed our heads and I said grace over the meal. After twenty-four years, we had a lot to be thankful for, and while we were praying, the server came. He waited until after I'd finished praying and said, "Are you Christians? I recently became a Christian. I love Jesus." Instead of an anniversary celebration, it became a three-way conversation, because the Lord is good.

When we love Jesus, it shows. It's hard to be a Christian and be mean to others or wear a scowl all the time. It doesn't matter what our old nature is, because "if anyone is in Christ, the new creation has come: The old has gone, the new is here!" (2 Corinthians 5:17).

Walking in the Footsteps of Ordinary Giants

Jesus called His disciples—His ordinary giants—to follow Him with excellence. God's Word and the Holy Spirit help us understand the depth and richness of the gospel—the good news of what Jesus has done for us. The first step in proclaiming the gospel with excellence is to dig deep into Scriptures and make this good news part of our lives. Then we can use Bible verses and our personal testimony to tell people about Jesus.

Once people become saved, Jesus calls them to live as His disciples. He gives us the command to go and make disciples of others. We do this with excellence when we follow Jesus with our whole hearts and live out what He taught. We teach others by example to listen and obey God's Word. An important part of discipling others with excellence is to gather with fellow believers to help each other grow as disciples.

Jesus wants us to live for Him with excellence in our daily lives. This translates to serving the Lord and others. We serve in visible and invisible ways as part of Christ's body, the church. Serving God helps us connect in meaningful ways with Him and with others. Part of our motivation to serve the Lord with excellence is to give something back to Him for all He has done for us. God gave us His best when He gave us Jesus. Will we choose to give our best back to Him and serve Him with excellence?

We look up to and admire people who do things well. Jesus' disciples were ordinary giants, people He called from every walk of life. They lived alongside Jesus for three years, learning how to live for God with excellence. Fully God and fully man, Jesus is the perfect example of an ordinary giant. Isaiah tells us, "He had no beauty or majesty to attract us to Him, nothing in His appearance that we should desire Him" (Isaiah 53:2). Yet, He lived a life of excellence—proclaiming the gospel of God's good news for everyone, making disciples, drawing people to worship and follow God, and serving others wholeheartedly.

There is no better person to have as captain of our ship. This most excellent captain will see us safely to shore. If we follow Him and live our lives for God with excellence, we can lead others to know and love our captain as well.

WORKBOOK

Chapter Seventeen Questions

Question: What comes to mind when you hear the word *excellence*? Who are some believers whose commitment to excellence has profoundly influenced your life?

_____

_____

_____

_____

_____

_____

_____

_____

_____

_____

_____

Question: Are you prepared to share the gospel with excellence? If not, how can you become confident in proclaiming the good news? What are some potential consequences of sloppy evangelism, and how does excellent evangelism honor Him and His Word?

_____

_____

_____

_____

_____

_____

_____

_____

_____

_____

Question: What are some priorities in your life—things into which you pour your heart and energies? (These might include a career, your home, your studies, or your family.) Do you demonstrate an equal passion and commitment to excellence as a disciple and servant of Christ? Make a list of some areas where you have grown lazy or apathetic in your Christian walk.

_____

_____

_____

_____

_____

_____

_____

_____

_____

_____

_____

Action: Look at your list above. For each area where you have not been walking with excellence, choose an action that you can begin to implement, such as a spiritual discipline, an accountability partner, or attendance in a small group. Ask God to renew your heart for excellence. Commit to giving Him your very best and to being an ordinary giant for Him.

Chapter Seventeen Notes

CONCLUSION

Walk in Faith

Those who have reached this page demonstrate they want to be ordinary giants for God. They want their lives to point to the One they look up to more than anyone else: Jesus Christ. He is the larger-than-life captain of their ship, and they trust Him to see them safely to shore. They want to make a difference and influence our world for Christ.

We've considered several examples of people who lived during the time of the early church in the New Testament. These Christians show us how to be ordinary giants in God's kingdom today. Each of these people of faith engaged with God and the people around them. They were willing to follow God with their whole hearts and become leaders for Him.

Leaders model and restore integrity.[60] The ordinary giants we've studied were people of strong character who were willing to be vulnerable. They weren't afraid to admit mistakes and start over. They understood the principle that they could influence others by practicing humility and letting God influence them and transform their lives. Jesus Christ was first and foremost in their lives; they trusted Him completely as their captain. This gave them the faith and resources to offer solutions to people who need God.

These ordinary giants invited people to meet and respond to Jesus. They influenced lives and built the kingdom of God because they:[61]

- Had authority from Jesus Christ to preach the gospel (1 Thessalonians 4:2).

- Invested in the lives of others without expecting anything in return.

- Trusted in God as the One true God.

- Showed kindness and mercy to others.

- Engaged in community with other believers through the fellowship they received from Jesus Christ (Philippians 2:1–2).

They put feet to their prayer—their conversation and relationship with God. They got off the pew and got working for God's kingdom. Ultimately, their actions influenced their world.

We've seen how God is faithful through the ages. Each of these ordinary giants exhibited courage and strength in some way. They used their unique abilities for God. He wants us to practice courage—the strength to go on in the face of fear and in the midst of the storms of life—today. God worked in all these great giants' lives. He had a plan for their lives, evidenced in their obedience and faithfulness to Him.

The first step to becoming ordinary giants who accomplish God's purposes is to walk with Him in faith. Our faith is the belief and certainty that Jesus gave up His life willingly to die in our place so that we might receive His mercy and forgiveness for sins if we call upon Him. God calls us all. He loves each of us and desires that we would follow Him (1 Peter 2:21). In our doubts, discouragement, and failure, God wants us as we are. He wants the people around us as they are.

Once we grasp the depth of God's love for us, we take the next steps to lead others to Him as we boldly share the good news of Christ's death on the cross. With God as the captain of our lives, He invites us to stand alongside Him and guide others safely to shore where they, too, can rest in His eternal salvation. We glorify God when we use our gifts and abilities to proclaim the gospel and reach out to others to invite them to meet Jesus.

With God, we stand in His strength and wisdom to influence the world and lead people to Jesus, our great Savior, one person at a time.

About the Author

French B. Harmon, Ph.D., is the President and CEO of the Kentucky Baptist Foundation, headquartered in Louisville, Kentucky. He has pastored growing churches for nearly thirty years. Harmon is a graduate of the Southern Baptist Theological Seminary, the University of Louisville, Marshall University, and the University of the Cumberlands. Dr. Harmon has recently completed the Executive Education program at Harvard University's Kennedy School of Government. He is married to Rachael, and together they have three children: Trae, Madison, and Jack. He is sports enthusiast, especially for baseball and his beloved Cincinnati Reds.

About Sermon To Book

SermonToBook.com began with a simple belief: that sermons should be touching lives, *not* collecting dust. That's why we turn sermons into high-quality books that are accessible to people all over the globe.

Turning your sermon series into a book exposes more people to God's Word, better equips you for counseling, accelerates future sermon prep, adds credibility to your ministry, and even helps make ends meet during tight times.

John 21:25 tells us that the world itself couldn't contain the books that would be written about the work of Jesus Christ. Our mission is to try anyway. Because in heaven, there will no longer be a need for sermons or books. Our time is now.

If God so leads you, we'd love to work with you on your sermon or sermon series.

Visit www.sermontobook.com to learn more.

REFERENCES

Notes

1 Schaetzle, Hayley. Email communication. July 6, 2017.

2 *Online Etymological Dictionary*, "gospel (*n.*)." https://www.etymonline.com/word/gospel#etymonline_v_9072.

3 Rogers, Adrian. In Connie Snow, *Sermon Notes, March 1973–February 2005*. Quoted in "Wit from Adrian Rogers." Artful Askers. https://www.artfulaskers.com/page/page/4718398.htm.

4 Warren, Rick. *The Purpose Driven Life*. Zondervan, 2009.

5 Murray, Andrew. *Humility: The Beauty of Holiness."* James Nisbet & Co., 1896, p. 94.

6 Osborne, Grant R. "Introduction to James." *ESV Study Bible*. Crossway, 2008, p. 2387.

7 Kunst, RC. "Interview: Andy Stanley with Summary Questions." Applied Truth. July 7, 2018. http://appliedtruth.org/interviews-1/2018/7/7/interview-andy-stanley-pt-1.

8 "All the Men of the Bible – James." Bible Gateway. https://www.biblegateway.com/resources/all-men-bible/James.

9 MacArthur, John. *Hard to Believe: The High Cost and Infinite Value of*

Following Jesus. Thomas Nelson, 2006, p. 2.

10 Blackaby, Henry T. and Claude V. King. *Experiencing God: Knowing and Doing the Will of God.* B & H Publishing Group, 2004, p. 261.

11 "Religion: Don v. Devil." *Time Magazine* L, no. 10 (September 8, 1947).

12 "Religion: Faith for a Lenten Age." *Time Magazine* LI, no. 10 (March 8, 1948).

13 Lennox, John. "How Many Nobel Prize Winners Believed in God." John Lennox (website). January 23, 2019. https://www.johnlennox.org/resources/145/how-many-nobel-prize-winners.

14 "All the Men of the Bible – Luke, Lucas." Bible Gateway. https://www.biblegateway.com/resources/all-men-bible/Luke-Lucas.

15 Lucado, Max. *The Gospel of Luke.* Thomas Nelson, 2006, p. vii.

16 "J. C. Penney." Christianity.com. https://www.christianity.com/church/church-history/timeline/1901-2000/jc-penney-11630672.html.

17 Wooden, Nan. "Faith, Love, and Basketball." Guideposts. February 18, 2011. https://www.guideposts.org/better-living/entertainment/sports/faith-love-and-basketball.

18 "Joe Gibbs: Leaving a Legacy." Christian Broadcasting Network. http://www1.cbn.com/700club/joe-gibbs-leaving-legacy.

19 Lucado, *The Gospel of Luke*, p. vii.

20 Cole-Rous, Jim. "Most Excellent Theophilus." Global Christian Center. https://globalchristiancenter.com/christian-living/lesser-known-bible-people/31472-most-excellent-theophilus.

21 Kennedy, D. James. *Why I Believe.* Thomas Nelson, 1999.

22 Kennedy, D. James. *The Gates of Hell Shall Not Prevail: The Attack on Christianity and What You Need to Know to Combat It.* Thomas Nelson, 1997.

23 Warren, Rick. "How to Use Your God-Given Influence As a Kingdom Builder." Charisma Leader. July 14, 2014. https://ministrytodaymag.com/leadership/counseling/21060-how-to-use-your-god-given-influence-as-a-kingdom-builder.

24 "Ancient Tax Collector." Bible History Online. https://www.bible-history.com/sketches/ancient/tax-collector.html.

25 Graham, Billy. *The Secret of Happiness.* Thomas Nelson, 2002.

26 "Rick Warren: 'God Didn't Need Us, He Wanted Us.'" Beliefnet. https://www.beliefnet.com/faiths/christianity/2005/10/rick-warren-god-didnt-need-us-he-wanted-us.aspx.

27 Barry, John D. "5 Ways to Really Live (and Give) Like Jesus." Crosswalk. https://www.crosswalk.com/church/giving/5-ways-to-live-and-give-like-jesus.html.

28 Moody, Dwight Lyman. *The Way to God and How to Find It.* F. H. Revell, 1884, p. 124.

29 Saint-Laurent, Jeanne-Nicole Mellon. *Missionary Stories and the Formation of Syriac Churches.* University of California Press, 2015, p. 17.

30 Brown, Steve. "Daring to Doubt: Learning from 'Doubting Thomas.'" Crosswalk. https://www.crosswalk.com/faith/spiritual-life/daring-to-doubt-learning-from-doubting-thomas-1110582.html.

31 Ortberg, John. "Walk on Water." Faith Gateway. September 1, 2014. https://www.faithgateway.com/walk-on-water/#.XPLnm4hKjtQ.

32 Stanley, Charles. "The Burden of Inadequacy" *In Touch with Dr. Charles Stanley.* Crosswalk. September 7, 2018. https://www.crosswalk.com/devotionals/in-touch/in-touch-sept-6-2010-11637568.html.

33 Swindoll, Charles R. *Moses: A Man of Selfless Dedication.* Great Lives Series, vol. 4. Thomas Nelson, 1999, p. 34.

34 Ranier, Thom S. "Six Evangelism Killers in a Church." Ranier on Leadership. July 21, 2017. https://thomrainer.com/2017/07/six-evangelism-killers-church-rainer-leadership-347/.

35 Zodhiates, Spiros. *The Complete Word Study Dictionary New Testament.* AMG Publishers, 1992, p. 3985.

36 Barclay, William. *The Gospel of John.* Vol. 1. Westminster Press, 1975, p. 202.

37 Henry, Matthew. *Matthew to John.* Vol. 5, Matthew Henry's Commentary

on the Whole Bible. Revised ed. MacDonald Publishing Company, 1721, p. 979.

38 Lutzer, Erwin W. *How in This World Can I Be Holy?* Moody Publishers, 1985.

39 Chandler, Matt. *The Explicit Gospel.* Crossway Books, 2014.

40 Zodhiates, Spiros. *The Complete Word Study New Testament.* AMG Publishers, 1991.

41 Greear, J. D. *Stop Asking Jesus into Your Heart: How to Know for Sure You Are Saved.* B & H Publishing Group, 2013, p. 48.

42 *Vocabulary.com Dictionary,* "enthusiasm." https://www.vocabulary.com /dictionary/enthusiasm.

43 Impelman, Craig. "Why Enthusiasm Is a Powerful Tool for Success." Success Magazine. April 19, 2017. https://www.thewoodeneffect.com /enthusiasm/.

44 "Nicky Cruz: Salvation in the Jungles of New York." Christian Broadcasting Network. https://www1.cbn.com/700club/nicky-cruz-salvation-jungles-new-york.

45 Wiersbe, Warren. *Be Mature (James): Growing Up in Christ.* David C. Cook, 1978, p. 37.

46 Severance, Diane. "John Newton Discovered Amazing Grace." Christianity.com. https://www.christianity.com/church/church-history/timeline/1701-1800/john-newton-discovered-amazing-grace-11630253.html.

47 Tozer, A. W. *What Ever Happened to Worship?* Christian Publications, 1985.

48 Idleman, Kyle. *Grace Is Greater: God's Plan to Overcome Your Past, Redeem Your Pain, and Rewrite Your Story.* Baker Books, 2017.

49 Henry, *Matthew to John,* p. 979.

50 Barclay, William. *The Gospel of John.* Vol. 2. Westminster Press, 1975, p. 263.

51 "The Extent of Fatherlessness." Fathers.com. http://fathers.com/statistics-

and-research/the-extent-of-fatherlessness/.

52 Evans, Tony. *Raising Kingdom Kids: Giving Your Child a Living Faith.* Tyndale House, 2016, p. 75.

53 Low, Robbie. "The Truth About Men and Church." Touchstone Magazine. https://www.touchstonemag.com/archives/article. php?id=16-05-024-v.

54 DeYoung, Kevin. "10 Principles for Christian Husbands and Fathers." The Gospel Coalition. April 14, 2015. https://www.thegospelcoalition .org/blogs/kevin-deyoung/10-principles-for-christian-husbands-fathers/.

55 Petruzzello, Melissa. "Magnificat." *Encyclopaedia Britannica.* https://www.britannica.com/topic/Magnificat.

56 Stanley, Andy (@AndyStanley). "Your greatest contribution to the kingdom of God may not be something you do but someone you raise." Twitter, April 17, 2013, 9:38 p.m. https://twitter.com/andy stanley/status/324713440541290498.

57 Blackaby, Richard. "Imparting Gifts." Experiencing God Day by Day. Blackaby Ministries International. December 17, 2018. https://blackaby.org/imparting-gifts/.

58 Brown, Kristine. "3 Things You Didn't Know About Mary (Mother of Jesus) in the Bible." Crosswalk. June 3, 2016. https://www.crosswalk.com/faith/women/3-things-you-didn-t-know-about-mary-mother-of-jesus-in-the-bible.html.

59 *Inspiration 365: Zig Ziglar's Favorite Quotes.* Sourcebooks, Inc., 2013, p. 6.

60 Crider, Alice. "Lesson 4, Module 2." Author Access MasterClass. https://www.alicecrider.com/author-access-masterclass.

61 Crider, "Lesson 4, Module 2."

Made in the USA
Middletown, DE
16 May 2021

39819727R00146